# Human Resource Development

## HRD-IR Interface Approach

# Human Resource Development

## HRD-IR Interface Approach

Sanjeev Kumar Singh

ATLANTIC

PUBLISHERS & DISTRIBUTORS (P) LTD

Published by
**ATLANTIC**
**PUBLISHERS & DISTRIBUTORS (P) LTD**
7/22, Ansari Road, Darya Ganj,
New Delhi-110002
Phones : +91-11-40775252, 23273880, 23275880, 23280451
Fax : +91-11-23285873
Web : www.atlanticbooks.com
E-mail : orders@atlanticbooks.com

Branch Office
5, Nallathambi Street, Wallajah Road,
Chennai-600002
Phones : +91-44-64611085, 32413319
E-mail : chennai@atlanticbooks.com



Printed in India at Nice Printing Press, A-33/3A, Site-IV, Industrial Area, Sahibabad, Ghaziabad, U.P.

*Dedicated to*

Gurudev Dr. Narayan Dutt
Shrimaliji
and My Father
Shri Ram Kumar Singh

# Contents

# An Administrator's Prayer

- Grant me the self-awareness to know honestly what I am, what I can do, and what I cannot.
- Grant me the judgement to channel my energies into those avenues which best utilise my abilities and do not require talents which I do not possess.
- Grant me the wisdom to cheerfully admit error and learn from my experiences, that I may grow and develop and avoid a repetition of mistakes.
- Grant me the humility to learn from others even though they be younger, less experienced, or of a humbler situation than I.
- Grant me the courage to make decisions whenever they are necessary and to avoid rashness when they are not.
- Grant me the sensitivity to judge the reactions of others that I may modify my actions to meet the needs of those affected.
- Grant me the perspicacity to acknowledge that I can be no more effective than my subordinates enable me to be, and to deal with them so that they can help me by helping themselves.
- Grant me the consideration to recognise the worth of each individual and to respect all those with whom I have contact, neither stifling their development nor exalting myself at their expenses.
- Grant me the tolerance to recognise mistakes as the cost of true learning, and stand behind my subordinates, accepting my responsibility for their actions.
- Grant me the insight to develop a personal philosophy, so that my life may have more meaning and satisfaction and that I may avoid capricious action under the pressure of expediency.

- Grant me the patience to live realistically with my circumstances, striving always for the better, but recognising the peril of a too rapid or a too drastic change.
- Grant me all these things, Dear Lord, that I may live a more useful life through the service of my fellow-men, and through them serve Thee.

(Katz, Robert L., "An Administrator's Prayer", *Harvard Business Review*, March-April, 1957, p. 40).

# Foreword

It is indeed a pleasure to foreword this brilliant book entitled *Human Resource Development* by Dr. Sanjeev Kumar Singh. The author deserves to be congratulated on outlining the multifaceted dimensions of Human Resource Development in a holistic lucid style and for his excellent effort in crystallising the essence of HRD. The pioneering research work contained in this book seeks to combine the emerging patterns of HRD distilled from research and insights by academicians, consultants and doyens of HRD.

Human Resource Development is a complex factor with the potential to play a very important role in the economic and social transformation of any country. HRD has received tremendous impetus as a result of the Liberalisation of National Economy. In recent years, the contribution of HRD to organizational and national competitiveness in international markets has been the subject of a large and growing literature. However, this pertinent book would be very useful for all those who believe in the basic philosophy of achieving results and lasting changes from trained and developed human resources.

This manual with a mission is bound to be of great relevance in an international market segment of management participants, research scholars, practising managers, HRD professionals and industries. The endeavoured and enriched parameters of HRD analysed in this book may further be utilized for promoting HRD, and Research and Development.

**B.N. Shukla**

Formerly University Professor & Head of the Department (Industrial Relations), Research Affiliate to Sydney University (Australia 1979), Visiting Fellow to Queen's University (Canada 1984), Consultant ICATVT (Turin, Italy 1984), Fellow IILS (Geneva), International Labour Organization (ILO) Functionary (Switzerland 1981-83)

# Acknowledgements

> "The love that asks no questions, the love that stands the test, the love that makes undaunted, The Final Sacrifice."

I express my deep gratitude to the versatile and most eminent professor, Dr. B.N. Shukla, Formerly University Professor — 'Industrial Relations' and Fellow IILS (Geneva) & International Labour Organization (ILO) Functionary (Switzerland), for sparing some of his precious time to write the Foreword for this book.

I place on record my immense indebtedness and gratitude to the doynes of HRM education in India — Prof. Subratesh Ghosh and Dr. S.N. Pandey whose writings have helped shape this book. I am also grateful to Fr. G.A. Hess, S.J., (Formerly Consultant, Xavier Institute of Management, Bhubaneswar) and Dr. P.K. Chakrabarti, Professor, Deptt. of Management Studies, Indian School of Mines, Dhanbad, for their valuable guidelines.

Thanks are due to all my teachers and colleagues in institutions and industries for their useful suggestions.

The preparation of this book has involved me to consult upon standard literature and journals both Indian and foreign for which I am obliged to the authors, editors and publishers of the works cited in the Bibliography and References. I am also obliged to the Authorities for permitting me to utilize their libraries.

The motivation for writing the book came from my affectionate mother, Late Uma Singh, who inspired me to pen this book. She taught me numerous useful things while still a child and probably the first lesson of management — "Never do things in a hurry or you will go wrong". My mother, whose smile alone conveyed a Blessing, would have been the happiest person to see the published book.

My father provided all sort of support and encouraged me to complete the manuscript despite considerable constraints and trying circumstances. He guided me with his experience and wisdom gathered over three decades in every conceivable situation in the arena of Man-Management and Industrial Relations.

I find myself at a loss of words to express my sentiments for my beloved wife Mrs. Rupa Singh, who suffered most on account of this book but stood by me in both light and shade, accepting the complete responsibility of my entire family. I am grateful to all my relatives and friends who have directly or indirectly helped me in bringing out this book.

"Radha Soami" to Prof. Yudhisthir Narayan Singh for his commendable efforts in completing the proofreading of the manuscript. He has always been there to help me maintain a proper perspective on life and living and, through his own creative talents, to inspire me to think in original and sometimes unconventional ways about the global problems of human resource development.

My Gurudev Dr. Narayan Dutt Shrimaliji provided me with the spiritual and intellectual inspiration to persevere under difficult circumstances for which I reaffirm my eternal devotion.

This book would not have seen the light of day without the cooperation of Dr. K.R. Gupta, Chairman, Atlantic Publishers & Distributors (P) Ltd., New Delhi. I would like to specially thank the editorial committee and record my appreciation for the team at Atlantic for their cooperation and help at every stage.

The book has been prepared with meticulous care. Yet any suggestions for the improvement of this book are always welcome and would be gratefully acknowledged.

**Sanjeev Kumar Singh**
E-mail: sks_3636@yahoo.co.in

# Overview

> "What a piece of work is man! how noble in reason! how infinite in faculty; in form and moving how express and admirable! in action how like an angel! in appreciation how like a God; the beauty of the world."
>
> —*Shakespeare*

Humans are unfathomable resources and all-embracing institutions. Human Resource Development is a dynamic and continuous process encompassing individuals, organizations and societies. HRD with its eclectic boundaries and multifaceted dimensions has been interpreted in various ways in different contexts and across cultures. In a simple and holistic manner, "HRD is concerned with creating a climate of work culture, productive efficiency and integration by building the capabilities of people; preparing them for change; improving productivity with quality development and achieving organizational goals in a dynamic and competitive business environment" (*India Journal of Training and Development*, Vol. XXVIII, No. 3).

We talk of the pre-eminence of human resources, but, in practice, we give it the lowest priority. Successful organizations and economies begin with people. Like revolution, innovations begin in the minds of men. Man, with his fertile imagination, has woven a network of activity and organization and he is its sole master. Man possesses a plethora of activities which fulfils his humanity from within, expresses his basic ideals, his dreams, his aspirations, his emotions and his values. Man is the basis of all unity, a fundamental bond of any substance or matter that exits today.

The skill and dexterity of manpower are in abundance in our country. The population has grown phenomenally, enlarging our workforce. Man cannot remain in complete isolation because he is aware that his needs, for which each individual is vying with every other, for power, prestige, recognition, appreciation, personal autonomy etc. cannot be fulfilled individually or even in a pair but in a society. It compels him, therefore, to join an organization to satisfy his economic, physical, social or spiritual needs. He establishes contacts with his peers, superiors and subordinates.

We are deluded by economic and technological viewpoints overshadowing our perspectives. The society, nay an organization, on the other hand, which is a combination of men, recognizes the supreme strength of the man. It recognizes that technology, the essence of civilization today, is not about tools only but demands complete involvement of men. An organization utilizes the human resources to fulfill its predetermined objectives. An organization predicts and controls the human behaviour, assesses its strength and impels man, who is a cog in the whole machine, i.e. an organization to give his best. In the present industrial world, one of the major tasks of management is to set and plan objectively, predict future steps, control and motivate the human force to achieve the predetermined goals. My attempt, therefore, while writing this book is to make you conscious of the importance of man, his development needs, his utilization and his motivation in the context of an organization.

Healthy and harmonious 'Industrial Relations' is an essential prerequisite for 'Human Resource Development'. Industrial Relations in a country are intimately connected with the form of its Government. The modern-day industrial relations scene in India is largely influenced by the legislative framework. Legislation concerning industrial relations in any country has to be seen in the light of the social, political and economic history of that land and the impact of contemporary events, both internal and external, that influence the evolution of that society. Society is dependent to a very large extent on the industrial world and society, and in turn the government therefore gets roped into this otherwise bilateral relationship.

Indian Industrial Relations have improved both in terms of verve and vigour. However, there is no estimate of colossal number of mandays lost due to underproductive and wasteful practices. The cause of major disputes in India concerns wages, bonus and allowances. Indian IR is vested in terms of profits, wages and dividends to the determinant of social and national interests. Long drawn legal battles and unsettled demands for wages prolonged for years, lead to frustration and low productivity, unrest and strife. To add to these road blocks, we have unions and associations which threaten to go on strike at the drop of a hat; politicians and bureaucracy that will promise to solve a problem only after it has reached crisis levels. We are more accustomed to think in terms of narrow identities like our own selves, our caste or community, linguistic groups. The problem is that we have not invested in educating people. We still seem to survive on the ignorance of our fellow citizens sometimes by deliberately keeping them ignorant so that they can continue to provide us gullible markets and vote banks. Trade union leaders and employers get busy in satisfying only their own selfish aims without a broader concern for the working class. This is undoubtedly an unhealthy sign.

The excessive influence of the industrial law on the life of an employer and also the employee is too not a healthy sign. However, the grip of statutes is such that in most enterprises the human factor in management is forgotten or ignored. This perhaps is inevitable in a country where healthy strong unions dedicated to the cause of workmen are rarely seen and the employers exploit the situation of politicized, multiple and weak unions. A plethora of industrial jurisprudence has not only created confusion but also has governed the industrial relations scene in this country. The influence of legislations is of such a magnitude that it has virtually replaced collective bargaining as a technique to settle disputes or resolve grievances. However, as and when the need to take a legal course arises, one needs to understand and appreciate the legal provisions in their true form and spirit in order that justice is done and objectives achieved. It should well be understood that legal provisions are meant to resolve the problems and settle the disputes and not aggravate them or precipitate matters. Obviously, solutions have to be found within the context of rather complicated laws but undoubtedly, psychological and sociological considerations play a very important role in management of human resources.

Management of 'Human Resource Development' and 'Industrial Relations' is a dynamic socio-economic process. Mutual respect and trust become the basis for any productive mutually beneficial and harmonious relationship. This is a socio-economic system based on the foundation of collaboration which ultimately results in the fulfilment of mutual needs. Like any other relationship this also goes through the alternate stages of conflict-collaboration-conflict and so on. In this dynamic ever-changing system, the parties are interdependent and therefore they must have an inherent desire for industrial harmony.

The coming years would witness an increasing trend towards HRD-IR interface for managing human resources, human relations, productivity and profitability in organizations. Therefore, additional topics on industrial relations interface have been incorporated in the book. Most of the eminent faculty members of professional management institutions, professors from universities, administrators, judicial experts and managers from industries are of the impression that the new paradigm of HRD-IR interface holds the key for survival, harmonious co-existence, work culture and wholesome development.

The silver lining can be seen in the efforts of organizations successfully adopting HRD-IR interface approach to manage their human resources. Surviving in a dynamic and competitive environment would require coping with market changes, employee involvements, productivity and quality targets, enhanced employee expectations and changing government policies. These can be achieved by introducing suitable HRD interventions and evolving HRD-IR interface to manage cooperation and conflicts at appropriate levels in the organization building process.

India does not suffer from resource gap, nor technology gap, nor planning gap; the real gap is the Human Resource Development gap. Our people are both an advantage and a disadvantage depending on how we behave. Experiences of structural adjustments undertaken by different countries in the last three decades have indicated beyond doubt that it is the "HRD factor" which makes the difference. Countries where structural adjustments are accompanied by right investments on developing people, have emerged as winners. The same analogy is true at the organizational level. Technological improvements, business strategies, quality concern etc., will have to be implemented through "Human Resources". What is required is not cheap manpower but skilled manpower, efficient manpower and achievement-oriented manpower. Men have to be galvanised, human resources have to be channellised, people have to be empowered through new skills, challenging jobs, open, trusting and demanding relationship to meet the future challenges. The development of a work culture based on the knowledge of the latest technology adopted to our needs and rich heritage can pave the way for further rapid development. Organizations, therefore, have to upgrade their work methods, work norms, technical and employee skills, and employee motivation to cope with the challenges. While there has been a great deal of concern with the environmental changes, the question of how organizations should develop their culture, skills and capabilities to meet the challenges has not been sufficiently addressed in terms of introspection, recharging and building new bases. We have to examine squarely our human assets, make human resources innovative, productive, committed and performing through appropriate HRD-IR interface in order to meet the challenges of global competitions.

*Human Resource Development* pertinently covers the syllabus of HRD and IR of Indian Universities at the level of MBA, MSW as also Post-Graduate Professional Programmes offering HRD and HRM in various Management Institutions. This book would also serve as a very helpful reference source for M.Com., CA and CS students and for those preparing for Management Trainee Tests and National Eligibility Tests (NET) for Lecturership in the area of Management. *Human Resource Development* would also be very useful guide for those aspiring for success in Union Public Service Commission (UPSC) examinations as it enables to develop cross-functional perspectives. This book would also be extremely valuable for Personnel & IR Managers, Training Managers, HRD professionals, Research scholars, Line Managers of Industries, Management consultants, Industrialists, Entrepreneurs and Business houses.

Concise presentation, content, coverage and practical inputs are the positive features of the work. Most of the available books on HRD tend to be theoretical and the management participant has to read between the lines to find the solution to the problems. *Human Resource Development* to a large extent succeeds in putting these "between the lines" solutions.

*Human Resource Development* would be valuable for all those who believe in the basic philosophy of achieving results and lasting changes from trained and developed human resources. We will have to be open to learning and taking a system and interdisciplinary approach to our work. Above all, we will have to boldly experiment and act. This book evolves a philosophy on HRD-IR interface approach relevant to our conditions from an experimental standpoint to underscore the need for giving high priority to HRD-IR interface for managing human resources, human relations, productivity and profitability in organizations. It is hoped that in the light of successes achieved by numerous companies both in the public and private sector, many more organizations would be willing to take up experiments in HRD-IR interface in the right earnest.

# Human Resource Development Climate: Interventions and Challenges*

1

India has the second largest pool of manpower in the world. Though humans are resources, they have to be trained and developed. Human Resource Development (HRD) is a dynamic and continuous process encompassing individuals, organisations and societies. The core of Management — 'the human core', is the essence of Human Resource Development. With this realisation increasing number of organisations are creating proper HRD divisions for developing their employees and managerial personnel. With economic liberalisation, comprehensive implementation of HRD programmes has become the order of the day for companies facing intense internal and global competition.

Development at times, can be a painfully slow process in our country with problems of poverty, unstability, illiteracy, technological inadequacies and industrial strife. Under the circumstances, HRD appears to be the main silver lining for resolving our problems and maladjustments in all spheres provided sufficient investments be made on it by the government, corporate sector and world bodies to make it more comprehensive and vibrant institution.

HRD with its eclectic boundaries and multifaceted dimensions is indeed difficult to define precisely. It has also been interpreted in various ways in different contexts and across cultures. However, we would try to define HRD in a simple and holistic manner as follows:

HRD is concerned with creating a climate of work culture, productive efficiency and integration by:

(i) Building the capabilities of people,

---

* This paper 'Human Resource Development Climate: Interventions and Challenges' by the author S.K. Singh has been published in *Indian Journal of Training and Development*, Vol. XXVIII, No. 3, July-Sept. '98 issue.

(ii) Preparing them for change,

(iii) Improving productivity with quality development and achieving organisational goals in a dynamic and competitive business environment.

Thus, apart from training and development dimensions with which it is generally associated, HRD interventions can be effectively used to achieve behavioural changes, work culture, productive efficiency, quality and integration. In the event of technological changes, HRD professionals can chalk out the appropriate leadership and motivation strategies. HRD interventions can also be used to develop and promote cross functional awareness. Integration can be achieved by co-ordination, team work, expression, participation, recognition and growth so as to reconcile employee satisfaction conducive to accomplishment of organisational goals.

The future manager more and more will become an educator. He will have to research, innovate, improve profitability, develop and live with the progress of technological change. The capabilities of Managers can be improved through HRD interventions such as: Action leadership, Operations Management Programme, simulators-laboratory, OD efforts, Management by Results (MBR) programme, cross functional task force, Budgeting and control, creating viable plans to cope with changes, quality upgradation programmes, external certification of internal processes and systems to assure quality like ISO-9000, quality circles, TQM, Kaizen system, demonstrating concern for employees, shared vision, programmes on self development and team building, value building processes and culture building interventions.

One of the characteristics of an excellent company is productivity through people. Productivity can be increased if it is linked with efficiency. HRD interventions (such as on-job-training, training for attitudinal change as well as for skill development, core competency building in multi-skill development, suggestion scheme, quality circles, cultural change of positive empowerment, participation and involvement, open communication and joint consultations, job enlargement and enrichment, job rotation, potential appraisal, employee satisfaction survey on HR policies and systems, promotion and welfare policies, programmes and actions to generate cost-consciousness, innovation, development of worker entrepreneurs, Juran quality improvement (JQI), training in quality management and retraining in the event of technological changes would go a long way in reorganising the workers and employees to cope with technological changes and maximising sales, productivity, quality, growth and greater customer satisfaction. Employee participation and participative management along with result oriented training for total employee involvement are recommended for achieving organisational development.

Organisational development would depend a lot on finding the optimum middle path by supplementing the use of:

(i) **Hard Technology**—Engineering techniques, physical structures, computers, modern machinery etc.,

(ii) **Soft Technology**—Human interactive processes, motivational techniques, participative planning processes, feedback etc.,

with the processes of:

(i) **Human Transformation**—Transcending the mind and its divisive tendencies, reconnecting with ones real self, meditation, attitudinal change, potential development for present/future roles, reconciliation of one's needs to perform within the organisational culture,

(ii) **Societal Consideration**—Pertaining to peripheral development, ecological balances, environment and pollution — for the general well-being and long-term sustainable society.

It is our conviction that human resource development system should emphasise on collective collaborations and address the needs and aspirations of employees in a humane and holistic manner. The challenge today for human resource development managers and facilitators is to create work culture that move the human spirit to excel.

It is our conviction that organisational rejuvenation can be made possible through HRD interventions and a HRD climate characterised by OCTAPACE (Openness, Confrontation, Trust, Authenticity, Proactivity, Autonomy, Collaboration, and Experimentation) culture with the following visible results (in some cases even quantifiable) in terms of:

(i) Emergence of a harmonious Industrial Relations climate.

(ii) High levels of motivation and trust.

(iii) Visibly higher initiative by workers.
(iv) Creative problem solving abilities amongst workers and innovation.
(v) Reduced absenteeism and better discipline.
(vi) Successful introduction of total quality management/ISO systems.
(vii) Successful retrenchment, redeployment and VRS schemes.
(viii) Foreign collaborations as sources of technology.
(ix) Reduced organisational stress.
(x) Cost reduction and waste elimination.
(xi) An urge to excel and client concern.
(xii) More cohesive team efforts.
(xiii) Greater sense of identification and pride in the organisation.

It is also our conviction that human resource development systems has to capture the workers' imagination, so as to optimize their strengths and energy systems (physical, mental and emotional) to make them capable of creative responses to complex industrial situations. In a business environment, where competition and not protection is the watch world, quality has become sine qua non for technological advancement. The challenge of HRD would be to create an environment of resilience which can accommodate and assimilate successfully changes in technologies, policies, methods etc., so as to reorient culture by getting individuals, teams and collectivities to feel a sense of belonging, commitment and mobilisation to welcome change in the interest of organisational transformation.

Surviving in a dynamic and competitive business environment would require coping with market changes; employee involvements; productivity and quality targets; enhanced employee expectations, and with changing government policies. These can be achieved by introducing suitable HRD interventions and evolving HRD climate to manage co-operation and conflicts at appropriate levels in the organisation building process.

# Human Resource Development and Liberalisation of Indian Economy

2

With liberalisation of the Indian economy, many changes are taking place in the corporate sector. There is pressure on Indian industries to perform, produce quality products and provide quality services. With increased competition, there is need to become cost-effective and efficient. There is also a need to improve technologies both in manufacturing and services. Organizations, therefore, have to upgrade their work methods, work norms, technical and managerial skills, and employee motivation to face up to the challenges.

The new economic environment has significance to all of us. First as citizens of this country, the next as responsible businessmen, leaders, managers and professionals and as users as well as providers of services. If the country has to get the best from the economic policies we all have to give our best and also get the best from each other. Every profession, discipline and function should contribute to make this happen. And HRD has a special responsibility as it deals with people.

According to Udai Pareek (1991), "Human Resource Development (HRD) is a new systematic approach to proactively deal with issues, related to individual employees and teams, and organizations and a movement to develop organizational capability to manage change and challenge."

We have to look at HRD from a broader and overall perspective. An economist views HRD from the economic angle of capital assets, labour productivity and skill formation. A psychologist's perception of the term borders on mental dimensions of attitudes, values, perceptions and intelligence. A sociologist's viewpoint might be quantum of social relations that is possible in the development process of the society.

Rao (1988) has defined HRD "as a system of frameworks, methods and processes aimed at systematically discovering, developing and using a person's capabilities to the fullest extent both for individual and organisational growth and well-being."

The process of developing human resources is done systematically by an organization to:

(i) Procure capabilities required to perform various functions associated with their present or expected future roles of the organization.

(ii) Improve their capabilities and discover and use their own potentials for their own and organizational development purposes.

(iii) Organize a culture in which supervisor-subordinate relationships, team work and collaboration among sub-units are strong and contribute to the professional well-being, motivation and pride of employees.

(iv) The HRD mechanisms and techniques include performance appraisal, counselling, training and organizational development interventions are used to initiate, facilitate, and promote this process in a continuous way.

(v) As HRD has no limit, the mechanisms need to be examined periodically. Organizations can facilitate this process of development by planning for it, and allocating organizational resources for the purpose.

Dynamic and growth oriented organizations do require HRD to succeed in a fast-changing environment. Organizations flourish only through the efforts and competencies of their human resources. Any organization will require HRD to develop the goals, sub-systems and beliefs of the organization to improve: the capabilities of individuals; the role of individuals; the attachment between management and the employees; co-operation among the departments; the overall environment of the organization that increases the capabilities of individuals, dyads, teams and the entire organization.

Normally, HRD systems would include the following mechanisms or sub-systems:

(i) Performance appraisal of employees.

(ii) Career planning of employees.

(iii) Training and development.
(iv) Quality management.
(v) Productivity improvement.
(vi) Improving quality of work life.
(vii) Rewards for achievement oriented performances.
(viii) Promoting team spirit and healthy industrial relations.
(ix) Periodic employee surveys and diagnosis of organizational health.
(x) Research and systems development.
(xi) Storing of Human Resources Information.

The sub-systems of HRD are linked with Human Resources Planning and strengthen other functions like Production, Marketing, Finance and Industrial Relations. The important environmental influences on Human Resource Development include demographic environment, economic, socio-cultural, political and technological environment.

The recent development in technology include Advanced Communication Systems, Industrial Robots, Flexible Manufacturing Systems, Computer Assisted Design (CAD) and, Computer Assisted Manufacturing (CAM). At the organizational level, technological improvements, business strategies, quality concerns etc., will all have to be implemented through people.

As a result of the various policy initiatives taken by the Government, India has been able to develop a very broad industrial base and an array of technological capabilities.

Baldev Raj Nayar (1983) in his analysis of the effects of Government policy on industrial and technological development writes, "...the overwhelming conclusion is the substantial, indeed awe-inspiring technological capability built in the country to serve as a base for technological independence or self-reliance. The bulk of industrial production in the country is based on the successful local assimilation and adaptation of technology or local generation of technology. The outflow of economic surplus on account of technology and licensing forms an insignificant proportion of its GNP.... The sources of technology have been fairly well diversified.... Because of the technological capabilities built up, India now largely breaks down 'the technology package', it selects what it wants and does not largely go in for turnkey projects, except perhaps in the case of projects sponsored by the World Bank...."

Since independence, India has laid heavy emphasis on self-reliance in all spheres of development and especially technology. Over the years, a solid diversified industrial base has been developed in the country. India has been hailed as one of the major countries in terms of industrial production. However, a continuous effort at technological upgradation would have to be launched to become internationally competitive in terms of cost and quality. Simultaneously, steps to develop requisite technological skills and those to design, develop and launch new products would be required.

Experiences of structural adjustments undertaken by different countries in the last two decades have indicated beyond doubt that it is the "people" who make the difference. Countries where structural adjustments are accompanied by right investments on developing people have emerged as winners.

The public policy orientation at the level of the centre is increasingly in favour of allowing the market forces to determine the course of developments in the economy as opposed to regulations and controls. Liberal attitudes towards acquisition of foreign collaborations have enabled not only the existing companies but also the new entrants to offer state-of-the-art technology and products. Concepts like privatisation and autonomy in the public enterprises are becoming realities in the Indian context. The attitude towards sick units is also changing from keeping them hanging to protect employment at any cost to allowing exit and providing alternative options for the displaced employees. The Central Government is also offloading a part of its investment in the Public Sector. The Government has reviewed the notion of public monopolies and has allowed private enterprise entry into the sectors that were otherwise reserved for the public sector. Making the public enterprises to operate in a competitive environment has put lot of pressure on them as they have not only to develop new competencies but also shed inefficient ones.

The HR profession and professional has an important role to play in helping organisations to develop appropriate HR strategies, in the wake of liberalisation of the Indian economy, in implementing such strategies and in managing the consequences of such strategies for the organization, its systems, structures, processes and its employees.

There is need to have a HRD function and activities that flow from organisational goals and mission. Where such goals and mission are not well articulated the function should design and use HRD systems to meet the various learning challenges posed and opportunities made available due to liberalisation.

# HRM & HRD Interventions and Achievements in Select Indian Companies

# 3

"Have you ever stood back and observed a proud parent check her child's first few steps? He takes a first awkward step, stumbles, looks up at her, sees her cheer, his eyes light up and with a gurgle of delight, takes yet another step." In organisations, this is what 'stretch principal', Management and success is all about.

Management is the efficient accomplishment of desired results in a given time frame, budget, environment through group efforts and involves the process of planning, organising, staffing, leading, controlling, co-ordinating material and human resources in a manner so that organisational objectives are accomplished. Human Resource Management (HRM) is concerned with — (i) Understanding the workforce to provide leadership; (ii) Developing their potentials to meet the needs of the organisation; (iii) Attracting and selecting suitable talent; (iv) Controlling, motivating and integrating the personnel employed; (v) Managing trade unionism, industrial relations, wages, welfare activities; and (vi) Foster a climate of productivity, team work and healthy labour management relations for the accomplishment of organisational objectives.

On the other hand, Human Resource Development (HRD) is concerned with creating a climate of work culture, productive efficiency and integration by: (i) Building the capabilities of people; (ii) Preparing them for change; (iii) Improving productivity with quality development and achieving organisational goals in a dynamic and competitive business environment.

Successful companies which hold the belief that Human Resource Development makes a difference have created proper HRD divisions for developing their employees and managerial personnel as is evident from the following list:

| Organisations | Significant HRM & HRD Interventions | Achievements |
|---|---|---|
| 1. SAIL (Steel Authority of India Ltd.) | On the job training, workers participation, information sharing, shop communication forums, unit training, shift to quality management. | Innovative thrust towards excellence. |
| 2. Infosys | Significant investment on Human Capital. | Achieving excellence in Knowledge Management. |
| 3. TISCO (Tata Iron & Steel Company) | Human resource orientation, open communication and joint consultations, supervisory training and education programme, training through simulation techniques, technicians and systems trainee schemes, collaborative ventures. | Continuous leadership and global player. |
| 4. VOLTAS | Total quality management, Juran quality improvement (JQI), cultural change of positive empowerment, programmes on self development and team building. | First Indian company to acquire the coveted ISO 9000 certification in all functions of manufacturing, marketing and servicing. |
| 5. ABB | Training for attitudinal change, awareness training in TQM, core competency building and multi-skill development, problem solving through small groups, total employee involvement. | World class company. |
| 6. ITC-ILTD | Induction of educated employees, multiple-skill training, changes in remuneration, promotion and welfare. | Organisational transformation. |
| 7. COAL INDIA LTD. (CIL) | Collaborations, quality circles. | Technological acquisition and development. |
| 8. BHARAT BHARI UDYOG NIGAM LTD. | Programmes and actions to generate cost consciousness. | Continuous improvement. |
| 9. DIAMOND & GEM DEVELOPMENT CORPORATION (& Scientific Diamonds Ltd.) | Development of worker entrepreneurs. | Human resource creativity and commitment. |
| 10. (i) STATE BANK OF INDIA (ii) BANK OF BARODA | Computerisation, consistency in discipline. | Customer client focus. |
| 11. (i) B.S.L. Co. Ltd. (ii) O.M.D. Co. Ltd. | Successful V.R.S. schemes | Restructuring of organisations. |

Contd...

| Organisations | Significant HRM & HRD Interventions | Achievements |
|---|---|---|
| 12. LARSEN & TOUBRO | Performance appraisal, counselling. | Achievement oriented culture. |
| 13. BHEL | Demonstrating concern for employees, Transactional analysis. | More cohesive team efforts. |
| 14. GODREJ (SOAPS LTD.) | Kaizen system, quality circles, 5-s (House Keeping). | Empowerment. |
| 15. (i) CROMPTON GREAVES<br>(ii) GUJARAT ESSAR<br>(iii) HOECHST | Shared vision, empowering. | Harmonious Industrial Relations Climate. |
| 16. (i) ASIAN PAINTS<br>(ii) PFIZER | Organization health diagnostic surveys. | Climate of Team Building. |
| 17. HEWLETT PACKARD | Customer surveys, focus groups, quality audits. | Organisational Effectiveness. |
| 18. TRANSPORT CORPORATION OF INDIA LTD. | Empowerment, performance assessment and review. | High levels of motivation and trust. |
| 19 (i) MARUTI UDYOG<br>(ii) RELIANCE<br>(iii) SEIMENS | Technology focus, energy focus, value analysis, value engineering, optimisation techniques. | Capable of meeting international competition. |
| 20. GUJARAT GAS COMPANY LTD. | Structured questionnaire, organisational health rating survey, personality, aptitude and the leadership profile tests, PPRD system (Performance Planning Review and Development System), drive for computer literacy amongst employees. | Sense of belongingness to the organisation. |

Some of the other companies with Human Resource orientation include ONGC, IPCL, CMC Ltd. and ICICI. The list is not exhaustive. Excellence through Human Resources Orientation have been achieved by the House of Tatas, Birlas, Thapars, Singhanias, Dalmias, Mafatlals, Reliance as also Market leadership by ACC, ABB, Godrej, Voltas, Bata, Modi Xerox, Marico, Eicher, ITC-ILTD, Thermax, Dr. Reddy's Laboratories, Hindustan Lever, Proctor & Gamble, Union Carbide, Videocon, and such global players like Philips, GM, IBM, HLL Citicorp, Citibank, Grindlays playing a major role in promoting HRD concepts and values.

It is heartening to note that even relatively smaller companies are in pursuit of achieving technology upgradation, harmonious industrial relations climate, total quality management and ISO 9000 accreditations through successful HRM & HRD interventions.

Successful organisations and economies begin with people. Like revolution, innovation begins in the minds of men. Every Indian agrees that India had a great past. Most Indians imagine that India has a great future, but what about the present? Anything you name, India produces and manufactures it, still it is at the crossroads. India does not suffer from resource gap; not technology gap, not planning gap, the real gap is the Human Resource Management gap. What is required is not cheap manpower but skilled manpower, efficient manpower, and achievement oriented manpower. Men have to be galvanised, Human resources have to be channellised; people have to be empowered through new skills, challenging jobs, open, trusting and demanding relationship. We have to examine squarely our human assets; make human resources innovative, productive, committed and performing through appropriate HRM & HRD interventions in order to meet the challenges of global competitions.

# Quality Management & HRD

# 4

In recent times, quality has emerged as one of the most important "Mantra" in organisations. In a business environment, where competition and not protection is the watchword, quality is the sine qua non for technological advancement. Quality improvement through technology upgradation and ISO 9000 certification and TQM have become the central themes for HRD activities. The fundamental assumption in Total Quality Management is that given the proper environment, systems and tools, people want to and will do their best. As Total Quality Management is essentially a people's process, HRD has a vital role to play in it. From the people context, Total Quality Management seeks to change entire work ethos for sustained high quality. The role of HRD in Quality Assurance System is threefold:

(i) To create awareness in all employees about it.

(ii) Building and maintaining training records, job fitness certification and collating of training needs from performance appraisals and other feedback mechanisms to draw training plan for future.

(iii) ISO 9000 being a continuous process, to meet requirements of training on an ongoing basis.

In the process of TQM transformation, the following major responses would be expected of union and management leadership:

(i) Establish the key players and responsibilities.

(ii) Establish a means for involving all union leadership in training, consulting and so on.

(iii) Identify the major areas that require the union's involvement.

(iv) Ensure that union leadership will be able to participate as planned.

It may be said that while TQM is concerned with culture, ISO 9000 is about systems.

The ISO 9000 series, developed by International Standards Organisation, Geneva, is a set of internationally accepted standards for a basic quality management system. The standards are designed to ensure customers that an organisation is using prescribed requirements of total quality. The five parts of the ISO 9000 series consist of three standards or models (9001, 9002 and 9003) and two guides (9000 and 9004).

ISO 9000 is a guide to the selection and use of Total Quality Management and quality assurance standards.

ISO 9001 is a standard for quality assurance in design and development, production, installation and servicing of products. This is clearly the most comprehensive standard.

ISO 9002 is a standard for quality assurance in production and installation activities.

ISO 9003 is a standard with a limited application for quality assurance in the final inspection and test activities.

The ISO 9000 series embodies comprehensive quality management concepts and guidance together with models for quality assurance requirements.

During the past years numerous organisations have acquired ISO 9000 accreditations and many more are in the pipeline.

All such organisations have spent thousands of man-hours in training employees to face ISO audit.

## Outstanding Features of ISO 9000

1. Using an integrated systems architecture, the ISO standards are packaged under a harmonised, easily memorised numbering system. These factors have high value in meeting the commercial and industrial needs of current international trade.

2. The standards can be applied with only minimal interpretation to any category of industry, *viz.* food, process or service besides manufacturing.

3. The standards are non-mandatory and non-dictatorial. They rarely prescribe condition. In most cases, it requires the company to establish its own procedures.

4. ISO 9000 envisages a meticulous documentation including preparation of quality policy, quality manuals, quality related procedures, job-instructions, audit reports and other quality records.

### Advantages of ISO 9000

The distinct advantages that accrue with the accreditation of ISO 9000 are:

- The biggest mandate for ISO 9000 probably comes from the accelerating competitive conditions in international markets with market imperatives virtually threatening to preclude those who miss the ISO 9000 bus. ISO 9000 is therefore not so much intrinsically advantageous as it is an impinging business reality of today.
- The concerted way in which ISO 9000 enforces quality discipline, institutionalising all basic ingredients of total quality, it uniquely makes possible the attainment of such quality levels which would not have been easily possible through other instruments.
- An important corollary benefit of having an ISO 9000 certification for any organisation is reduction of the costs of multiple assessments by multiple trading partners.
- Today, ISO 9000 has come up as a very potent marketing tool to demonstrate the supplier's commitment to quality.
- An assortment of beneficial outcomes activating various organisational improvements within becomes possible with ISO 9000. One, it smoothens out procedural irritants and irregularities and makes operations more even and predictable. Two, establishment, adoption and maintenance of detailed work procedures opens up new frontiers for employee's involvement. Finally, through its independent audit and management review clauses the standard makes way for horizontal and bottom upward lines of communication.
- Accreditation to ISO 9000 potentially mitigates product liability cases also. Many insurance companies providing liability indemnity policies offer reduced premiums to registered organisations.
- Our EXIM Policy 1992-97 gives certain benefits in the form of special import license to industrial organisations having ISO 9000 certification.

### Drawbacks of ISO 9000

- The implementation of a formal quality system is very demanding of resources and ISO 9000 in particular has substantial cost implications. Although it is improbable that any company which has been in competitive business for some time, would be without a system, the finalisation and documentation of the system is time consuming and may substantially escalate administrative set-up and expense. Assessment and registration are also costly.
- It follows from this that unless carefully planned and continuously adhered to, the system may turn out to be cost ineffective and cumbersome.
- The kind of changes in work attitudes and work practices that the standard envisions are too daunting and may over tax the already strained management capabilities, making the whole venture unproductive.
- Most of the organisations have already committed heavily in terms of physical and financial resources towards building quality into their set up. Many have progressed considerably on the TQM road. These endeavours may not be perfectly compatible with the requirements of ISO 9000. If this were so, climbing the ISO 9000 bandwagon now may mean a fresh commitment of resources and therefore wasteful.
- Although registration of a company to ISO 9000 is expected to eliminate second party assessments, this may not happen in practice in the long run. As the ISO net spreads far and wide, it is more likely that a purchaser will use the standard as a guide to indicate those companies it is worth looking at more closely, given that by then, mostly of them would be on ISO stream.
- Traditionally, most trade unions have not been recognised as ardent champions of work systems and standards. It may be extremely difficult for them to wholeheartedly accept strict and continuous adherence to systems and work procedures—ISO 9000 would thus mean for management, a long war of attrition with such unions.

The strongest hurdle in implementation of Total Quality Management is that there is no concrete formula. It is going to be a real challenge to HRD professionals to train, retrain and seek employee involvement and participation in pursuit of TQM despite unpalatable realities. Since quality will have direct bearing on survival of organisations and thereby its employees, even unions in principle cannot afford to resist this concept per se as quality has emerged such a superordinate goal for all in today's competitive business environment.

Another powerful HRD intervention namely the Quality circle is basically a small group to perform quality control activities voluntarily within the same workshop. "In the original concept of Quality circle, the word 'voluntary' is interpreted in the Japanese context of language and culture where it means 100% participation". Reason for using the word "voluntary" rather than the word "compulsory" is that there is permission to vary the quantum of work done by the circle. The Japanese appreciated that problem solving (which is what the circles do) needs creativity, and technology is not available to generate creativity on a day to day basis. Hence the permission to change work processes. The Indian interpretation of quality circles, done out of context, has resulted in a powerful technique yielding poor results.

And total quality management is inculcation of total quality culture with total participation and various means as ISO 9000, Quality Circles, HRD and so on to catalyse and institutionalise it. Quality Management is not an overnight phenomenon. It takes time and at marketplace there is no time in buyers market where customer is king. Thus, organisations have to strike golden balance to achieve best of the both worlds.

# Human Resource Development for Workers

# 5

The fact that workers represent the largest organised segment of the country heightens the need for HRD for workers. And so HRD has to advance from managerial development to worker development and tuned to ground realities. Some of the Japanese techniques can be useful in developing workers in the Indian context. These include (i) Morning prayer meetings, (ii) Kaizen, (iii) Housekeeping or 5s, and (iv) Quality circles.

Based on the pillars of education, training and knowledge, some of the areas in which HRD professionals can develop workers are as follows:

1. **Spreading Awareness regarding Accident Prevention and Safety.** In our country, increasing number of human lives are being lost due to industrial accidents. "Industrial accidents are the end products of unsafe acts and unsafe conditions of work. Accidents are preventable, they do not just happen. They usually occur as a result of the combination of number of factors in which technical equipment, working environment and 'fatigue' are important. Six of the main reasons which causes 'fatigue' amongst workers are: (i) worry, (ii) grief, (iii) ill health, (iv) bad temper, (v) frustration and (vi) intoxication. Taking head load of this burden, it is likely that the worker will meet an 'accident'. Amongst the factors contributing to safety awareness and accident prevention are: (a) persuasion, (b) regulation, (c) education, (d) vigilance, (e) equipments, (f) nutrition, (g) training, (h) inspection, (i) observation, and (j) nature.

2. **Spreading Awareness regarding Occupational Health.** There are factors in the workplace that affect the health of the workers. Occupational health has various departments such as occupational physiology, industrial safety, ergonomics, occupational psychology, industrial hygiene especially in relation to Toxicology and Industrial

Medicine. Various occupational diseases can be grouped under the following:

(i) Occupational lung disorder, e.g., pneumoconiosis, arthracoces, asbestosis etc.

(ii) Severe traumatic injuries on accident, e.g., fracture crush injury etc.

(iii) Musculo skeletal disorder, e.g., sprain, ligamental tear, backache, etc.

(iv) Occupational cancer of skin, lungs etc.

(v) Occupational neurotoxic, e.g., lead, mercury, manganese.

(vi) Noise induced hearing loss.

(vii) Occupational dermatology, e.g., dermatitis, eczema.

(viii) Psychological disorders, neurosis hypertension etc.

Apart from these, early diagnosis and treatment of case findings of Malaria, TB, Hypertension and Diabetes is recommended.

Previously known as industrial health, the father of occupational medicine Bernadeno Ramazzine's statements which bear repeating are:

(A) All physicians should ask their patients without fail, of what trade they do.

(B) Learn the nature of the occupational diseases by visiting the place of work with regard to:

  (i) Prevention of departure from health due to their working condition.

  (ii) Protection of workers from factors in the workplace that affect health.

  (iii) Maintenance of highest degree of physical, mental and social well-being.

The Government, employer, workers and health personnels are responsible for occupational health. Therefore, health care to the workers in special reference to their occupation and knowledge about the hazards of the occupation they are working in along with safety equipments and first aid facilities are essential.

3. **In Areas of Counselling Workers.** If a big organisation sincerely takes up a programme of promoting worker entrepreneurs or training its labour in setting up small units that can produce items

which can be supplied to the parent unit, many workers will be willing to quit the mainstream to take up their own ventures. In this regard, the Japanese industries particularly in the textile sector follow a unique programme for their women employees. They are simultaneously taught vocations which they can pursue after their marriage in the event of quiting the company. The result is that they do not have a fear psychosis of losing a job.

Counselling workers to make rationalization of labour less painful with their emphasis on retraining and redeployment, helping them in skill development, helping them to start some business on their own after termination or retrenchment, guiding them in proper investment of the money they get under VRS as also to help them branch out to new areas and vocations with positive approach would be the real challenges of HRD departments in relation to workers as also to other categories of employees.

Counselling also helps in improving discipline which is necessary to maintain orderliness. Problems like late coming, disobedience, wilful absenteeism, drunkenness while on duty can be rectified by:

- Private counselling advising the employee to change his habits.
- Verbal counsel by explaining the consequences of failure to heed the advice being rendered.
- Counselling in writing and issuing warnings asking him to explain his conduct.

Lay-off, downgradation or discharge of employees should not be hurriedly exercised without building up a case even if it is within the competence of the manager.

Sometimes an employee, because reasons such as family difficulties, health, financial imbalance, social commitments, housing, etc., may be tense and is not able to concentrate on his work.

He may feel greatly relieved if there is some superior in whom he can confide or whose advice he can seek. The counsellor should be a person who is trained to listen, counsel and try to report to the management facts without either embarrassing the employee or making a commitment to him. Sometimes little help or coordination enables him to get over the situation or his confused way of thinking. He may feel grateful and regain his failing interest in his work.

Such counsel may not necessarily always bring good results. Sometimes it may result in an adverse decision depending on how the counsellor has handled a situation.

An employee may be subjected to many outside and inside forces stimulating or vitiating his mental condition or working efforts. Some typical negative forces are:

- Mental condition arising out of failure to achieve some desired/coveted aim, loss of a member of the family, housing, etc.
- Defeatist attitude arising out of his failure at work, love, home life (placing his attitude towards work).
- Physical condition causing temporary setbacks, or aging or some emotional instability.
- Change of interest leading to wishful thinking, desire for change and so on.

Some of the corrective measures that may emerge from counselling are:

- Self-realisation of the forces acting on the individual.
- Change in work and habits.
- Outlets for repressed desires.

In case the immediate supervisor has the calibre to handle such cases he should do so or the HRD manager or his assistants can play this role more effectively.

Some of the useful Japanese techniques for developing workers and employees in the Indian context include morning prayer meetings, Kaizen, housekeeping or 5s and quality circles:

**1. Morning Prayer Meetings.** The morning prayer meeting is an excellent starting point for bypassing much of the suspicion between union and management and is guaranteed to be available everyday. The morning prayer would generally not be resisted as it is a brief one called ostensibly to cheerfully charge up subordinates for the days work on a sentimental and religious note. It can effectively be used as a communication channel and helps in scheduling and prioritizing the days work, set targets, with the help of everybody relating to visible results at the workplace. The morning prayer may deal with solving small irritants and quick problem solving at the instance of the boss but big problems are not to be solved here and should not dig into 'why' and 'who' — thus finding fault for a past event and demotivating people. Its limitation may be that of time (although brief) but its impact goes beyond the days work.

**2. Kaizen.** Kaizen is based on the principle of empowerment of employees by recommending improvements with zero financial investment thus stimulating creativity. Necessity being the mother of invention, inventiveness surfaces rather than from the investment made with additional outlay resulting in saving of resources and simple solutions to complex problems. Kaizen opens up channels of positive communication, where good work done by employees is reported upwards on a regular basis, the workers getting appreciation and rewards for their creativity, improvements done and talents.

**3. Housekeeping or 5s.** It is a powerful strategy to bridge the gap between the workers and management. Housekeeping reduces maintenance costs, discarded what we do not need, such as the reuse of scrap, releases resources, 5s, unites people and releases resources.

**4. Quality Circles.** As the crux of quality circle movement lies in its voluntariness, it is essential that the programme evokes initiative and participation from employees. There has to be 100% participation. Similarly, the management should participate in setting targets, problem solving, tools and techniques, and contributing ideas for the quality circles.

Once the QC mechanism is in place a number of new techniques can be taught through it like value analysis, Kepner-Tregoe method, new 7 tools etc. and the path to development for workers gets opened up.

## Improvement in the Quality of Working Life

A particular movement for improving the motivation to work which has attracted considerable attention in recent years depends on the 'Improvement of the Quality of Working Life'. Several experiments on this approach have been carried out in Norway, Sweden, the USA, India and Japan.

The essence of this approach to improve the Quality of Working Life lies in its emphasis on the changes in the socio-technical system of work through improvements in the work design, working environment and conditions, organisation of work, hierarchical structure and the production process brought with the active involvement of workers in decision making. The approach relies a good deal on the internalised motivation including job enrichment, but does not exclude or minimise hygienic factors. Nitish De, an important protagonist of this movement in India, emphasised the relevance of some hygiene factors in the course of his experiments on work design in India. He found work layout, working conditions and facilities for supply of inputs as some of the visible irritants to the workforce during the operation of his participative redesign projects in three Indian organisations. According to him, in the work redesign approach the emphasis is 'on creating an ongoing urge for an improved quality of working life' among the workers. As a result of this improvement, productivity gains are achieved. But that is not the main objective of the movement. The principal objective, on the other hand, is to generate a participative culture in the workplace. This is expected to bring change in attitude to work by accommodating employment policies and operating practices to the rising expectations of employees. The changes in attitudes would bring more commitment to work and job satisfaction and are expected to contribute to the rise in productivity. Thus essentially the thrust of the movement for the improvement in the Quality of Working Life is on the internalised motivation.

### Quality of Worklife

Quality of worklife improvements are defined as "any activity which takes place at every level of an organisation, which seeks greater organisational effectiveness through the enhancement of human dignity and growth...a process through which the stakeholders in the organisation management, unions and employees — learn how to work together better...to determine for themselves what actions, changes and improvements are desirable and workable in order to achieve the twin and simultaneous goals of an improved quality of life at work for all members of the organisation and greater effectiveness for both the company and the unions."

Richard E. Walton explains quality of work life in terms of eight broad conditions of employment that constitute desirable quality of work life (QWL). He proposed the same criteria for measuring QWL. Those conditions/criteria include:

(i) **Adequate and Fair Compensation.** There are different opinions about the adequate compensation. The Committee on Fair Wages defined fair wage as "...the wage which is above the minimum wage but below the living wage."

(ii) **Safe and Healthy Working Conditions.** Most of the organisations provide safe and healthy working conditions due to humanitarian requirements and/or legal requirements. In fact there conditions are a matter of enlightened self-interest.

(iii) **Opportunity to Use and Develop Human Capacities.** Contrary to the traditional assumptions, QWL is improved... "to the extent that the worker can exercise more control over his or her work, and the degree to which the job embraces an entire meaningful task"...but not a part of it. Further QWL provides for opportunities like autonomy in work and participation in planning in order to use human capabilities.

(iv) **Opportunity for Career Growth.** Opportunities for promotions are limited in case of all categories of employees either due to educational barriers or due to limited openings at the higher level. QWL provides future opportunity for continued growth and security by expanding one's capabilities, knowledge and qualifications.

(v) **Work and Quality of Life.** QWL provides for the balanced relationship among work, non-work and family aspects of life. In other words, family life and social life should not be strained by working hours including overtime work, work during inconvenient hours, business travels, transfers, vacations, etc.

(vi) **Social Relevance of Work.** QWL is concerned about the establishment of social relevance to work in a socially beneficial manner. The workers' self-esteem would be high if his work is useful to the society and the vice versa is also true.

### Specific Issues in QWL

Trade unions claim that they are responsible for the improvement in various facilities to workers whereas management takes credit for improved salaries, benefits and facilities. However, HR managers have identified specific issues in QWL besides normal wages, salaries, fringe benefits etc., and takes lead in providing them so as to maintain higher order QWL. Klott, Mundick and Schuster suggested 11 major QWL issues. They are:

(i) **Pay and Stability of Employment.** Good pay still dominates most of the other factors in employee satisfaction. Various alternative means for providing wages should be developed in view of increase in cost of living index, increase in levels and rates of income tax.

Stability to a greater extent can be provided by enhancing the facilities for human resource development.

(ii) **Occupational Stress.** Stress is a condition of strain on one's emotions, thought process and physical condition. Stress is determined by the nature of work, working conditions, working hours, pause in the work schedule, worker's abilities and nature and match with the job requirements. Stress is caused due to irritability, hyper-excitation or depression, unstable behaviour, fatigue, stuttering, trembling, psychosomatic pains, heavy smoking and drug abuse. Stress adversely affects employee's productivity. The HR manager, in order to minimise the stress, has to identify, prevent and tackle the problem. He may arrange the treatment of the problem with the health unit of the company.

(iii) **Organisational Health Programmes.** Organisational health programmes aim at educating employees about health problems, means of maintaining and improving of health etc. These programmes cover drinking and smoking cessation, hypertension control, other forms of cardiovascular risk reduction, family planning etc. Effective implementation of these programmes result in reduction in absenteeism, hospitalisation, disability, excessive job turnover and premature death. This programme should also cover relaxation, physical exercise, diet control etc.

(iv) **Alternative Work Schedules.** Alternative work schedules including work at home, flexible working hours, staggered hours, reduced work week, part-time employment which may be introduced for the convenience and comfort of the workers as the work schedule which offers the individual the leisure time, flexible hours of work is preferred.

(v) **Participative Management and Control of Work.** Trade unions and workers believe that workers' participation in management and decision making improves QWL. Workers also feel that they have control over their work, use their skills and make a real contribution to the job if they are allowed to participate in creative and decision-making process.

(vi) **Recognition.** Recognising the employees as a human being rather than as a labourer increases the QWL. Participative management, awarding the rewarding systems, congratulating the employees for their achievement, job enrichment, offering prestigious designations to the jobs, providing well-furnished and decent workplaces, offering membership in clubs or association, providing vehicles, offering vacation trips are some means to recognise the employees.

(vii) **Congenial Worker-Supervisor Relations.** Harmonious supervisor worker relation gives the worker a sense of social association, belongingness, achievement of work results etc. This in turn leads to better QWL.

(viii) **Grievance Procedure.** Workers have a sense of fair treatment when the company gives them the opportunity to ventilate their grievances and represent their case succinctly rather than settling the problems arbitrarily.

(ix) **Adequacy of Resources.** Resources should match with stated objectives, otherwise, employees will not be able to attain the objectives. This results in employee dissatisfaction and lower QWL.

(x) **Seniority and Merit in Promotions.** Seniority is generally taken as the basis for promotions in case of operating employees. Merit is considered as the basis for advancement for managerial people whereas seniority-cum-merit would generally be preferred. The promotional policies and activities should be fair and just in order to ensure higher QWL.

(xi) **Employment on Permanent Basis.** Employment of workers on causal, temporary, probationary basis gives them a sense of insecurity. On the other hand, employment on permanent basis gives them security and leads to higher order QWL.

*QWL and Fringe Benefits.* HR managers have to build and maintain QWL providing a wide range of fringe benefits. Fringe benefits and social security benefits result in improvement in productivity, reduction in absenteeism, turnover, sick leave, alienation etc. These benefits or maintenance activities include medical and health benefits, safety measures, legal and financial services, consumer services, retirement's benefits, conveyance, canteen facilities, recreational services, career counselling, employee's information reports etc.

*QWL and Productivity.* The general perception is that improvement in QWL costs much to the organisation. But it is not so, as improvement over the existing salary, working conditions and benefits will not cost much. However, the rate of increase in productivity is higher than that of cost of QWL. Thus increase in

QWL results in increase in productivity. But continual increase in QWL eventually leads to reduction in productivity due to increase in cost of output. This is because the worker's output does not increase proportionately after a certain level, even though QWL increases.

Improved QWL leads to improved performance. Performance should mean not only physical output but also the behaviour of the worker in helping colleagues in solving job related problems, accepting orders with enthusiasm, promoting a positive team spirit and accepting temporary unfavourable work conditions without complaint.

The typical Indian worker sees himself as a victim of circumstances. He has come to believe that management is only interested in his output and not in his welfare. Sometimes, the unions are 'bought over' by the management and on their own, the unions rarely arrange training programmes for workers. They tend to believe that an uneducated worker is easier to lead — from fear of workers being brainwashed by the management through training, learning mechanism and other OD interventions.

Our country, which has the second largest pool of manpower in the world has borrowed heavily from the World Bank and is continuing to borrow. The only way we can repay is by generating enough to repay. This would require among other factors, substantial investment in areas of training and educating workers to improve their efficiency. HRD for workers can also help achieve our socio-economic objectives and tackle the problems of poverty and illiteracy — translating directly into quantifiable returns.

A change from one of suspicions and conflicts to one of collaborative workings will certainly require attention, encouragement, financial investments and time as also transformation in the attitudes and roles of management and employee unions. But the effects can be lasting as numerous Indian companies experimenting and successfully implementing HRD techniques have shown and brought to the realisation, the focus on 'Human Core' — Thankfully! now more organisations seem to be willing to undertake HRD for workers.

# Human Resource Planning 6

Human Resource Planning involves an analysis of the existing manpower, their skills and capabilities, as well as an understanding of the future requirements of the organization. The effective utilisation of the personnel by developing them according to the changing requirements is also inevitable. Planning is essential regarding the surplus personnel also.

Human Resource Planning has been defined as 'the strategy for acquisition, preservation, improvement and utilisation of company's Manpower resource'. It actually refers to the application of the planning process for employing the right number of personnel of the right type and for utilizing them in a planned manner to meet the corporate goals. For this purpose, manpower demand forecasts for the planning period are to be made. These are then compared with the forecasts of manpower supply. Then plans are made for achieving the balance between supply and demand and also for proper utilisation of the personnel to be employed in future.

Every organization has its 'output' although this may not be cardinally measurable in each case. Whatever may be the measure of human effectiveness used in an organization, Human Resource Planning can make substantial contribution to improve it. Even in other cases, 'output' would mean the results of the productive efforts of the organization. The absolute level of output, or work, or service is important to an organization, in order to understand the level and extent of manpower utilization, a measure of output in relation to the manpower-input utilized may be more useful. Such a ratio is what productivity measurement implies. For the organizations in which output is cardinally measurable, the productivity of labour can be a very useful indicator of the effectiveness of manpower per man-hour (net output or net value added per man-hour).

In organizations where precise qualitative measurement of manpower productivity is not practicable, an approximate idea of the level of manpower effectiveness can be had from the relevant objective indicator of the work achieved per man-hour. Some other alternative measures of effectiveness in similar cases may be the cost per unit of man-hour (a reduction of which for the same level of work or output indicates better efficiency), or time used or saved per man-hour.

In some organizations, labour cost is important element in the total costs. In some others, although not the dominant one, it is one of the major elements of costs. Whatever is the case, an excessive rise in labour costs, without any corresponding benefits to the organization, would definitely affect the total costs and, therefore, the prices and the competitive effectiveness of the unit in the market.

In this connection it is necessary to remember that the labour costs do not depend only on wages paid out to the workers. There are several other elements of labour costs which are not received by the employees, but are to be incurred for employing them. Important illustrations of the later categories are the welfare expenditures for workers, benefits in kind to employees, costs of recruitment, incidental expenses for employment, employer's contributions to social security measures etc.

If the demand-supply comparison of the manpower categories identifies manpower surplus, it may become a potential problem. The main approaches which may be followed to meet the problem of surplus in specific categories of manpower are re-deployment in the form of transfers, or long-term orientation or training, or retrenchment or attrition (i.e. long-term policy of keeping the vacancies caused by retirement unfilled).

There are practical constraints in terms of labour-relations, Government legislations, or policy in following the last alternative, apart from the social and human considerations. All possible care has to be taken to find out whether the surplus people can be absorbed (may be after some short-term training or orientation in some other expanding activities or departments of the organization), where there may be shortage of manpower.

If the possibilities are closed in that respect, the long-term manpower requirements of the organization have to be considered on the basis of the long-term Human Resource Plan and objectives of the organization.

If it is not immediately possible to absorb these surplus personnel, they may be sent for long-term training to equip them for future requirements, possibly on the same basic pay, but without some of the allowances.

Over a certain length of times, these measures may substantially reduce the surplus, depending on the age-composition of the relevant employees.

But if none of these efforts succeeds and a decision for separation from the surplus employees has to be taken, they may be offered the option of voluntary retirement or substantial compensatory benefits (e.g., an attractive gratuity or a percentage of the basic pay as pension) which should compare favourably to the statutory retrenchment-compensation payable to the worker.

Such a policy may avoid much of the industrial frictions and may reduce the bitterness which is usually associated with separations before the due time or retirement.

The organizations which operate with 'corporate planning system' consciously and precisely spell out their objectives, both short- and long-term. In other organizations in which such systematic corporate planning procedures are not observed, the top management have in their minds some goals which they like to achieve at least in the immediate future, although these may or may not be announced or shared with others.

The success of an organisation would depend primarily on the quality and the number of personnel procured by the organization, the way they are utilized and the extent to which tools and methods are developed for achieving the corporate objectives. The study of Manpower Sciences is young, having teething troubles, yet is being practised by many organizations successfully.

Above all, Human Resource Planning influences the restructuring of the organization through the following three stages as brought out by M.B. Athreya:

(i) *Cost Awareness.* At least taking interest, measuring and knowing the actual costs relative to benefits, of all activities, equipment materials, systems and practices.

(ii) *Cost Control.* Going a step further, setting norms or standards for all costs, measuring actuals, identifying variances, analysing and taking corrective actions, either to meet or exceed the standards.

(iii) *Cost Reduction.* The third stage of periodically challenging the standards themselves through value analysis, value engineering etc., and tightening the standards. Apart from 'Manpower costs', Human Resource Planning helps upgrade the cost benefit management skills of all functions like project, design, materials, manufacturing, maintenance and auxiliary services, through inputs in value analysis, value engineering and other optimisation techniques.

Technology progression is inversely proportional to the manpower requirement. Thus, Human Resource Planning is also looked upon as cost optimisation option.

Some of the important factors affecting Human Resource Planning at the local level (operating through the local labour market) are:

1. Population density at various distances from the factory or the workplace.
2. Local unemployment level, particularly of the categories which are relevant for the operation of the organization.
3. Availability of part-time labour.
4. Current competition for the similar categories of manpower from other organisations, both local and national.
5. Potential pulls from the competing organisations with respect to the similar categories of manpower.
6. Output from the local educational system (general as well as technical or specialised).
7. Pattern of immigration and emigration within the area and between it and other areas.
8. Residential facilities available now and in future.
9. Local transport facilities and commutation pattern.

In addition to these, certain other factors operate from the national level on the manpower supply at the corporate level. Special mention may be made of the following:

1. Trends in the growth of the working population.
2. Government training schemes and systems of technical, vocational, professional and general education.
3. Mobility of the products of the technical, professional and vocational institutions.

4. Impact of social security measures of certain types, e.g., unemployment benefits, lay-off and retrenchment benefits, etc., on the manpower supply.
5. Cultural factors and customs, social norms etc., affecting school leaving age, labour force participation of women, children and young persons capable of joining educational institutions as students.

## Executive Resource Planning

There are four major elements in the process of executive resources planning that would claim the attention of the companies:

- Executive resources inventory.
- Executive resources forecasting.
- Career development plans.
- Management succession systems.

Executive resources planning is concerned with the implementation of the basic human resources objective of having the right people in the right places at the right time. Viewed in this light, the activities necessary to implement executive resources planning become as much an integral part of the human resources function as any other activity in the human resources development.

The need for a practical approach to executive resource planning is based on the obvious requirements of the organisation situation. As many companies are aware, the situation calls for advance planning and preparation with respect to executive manpower in much the same way it does with respect to buying and selling.

## Executive Resources Inventory

As a starting point, for executive resources planning in a company, information about future requirements would be just worthless unless accompanied by adequate information about present executive resources. In addition to knowing how many executives there are in the company, in various categories and levels, we must find out in detail many other relevant aspects. In planning future utilisation of manpower particularly at the managerial level, it is not enough to know that the present executive calibre is made up of so many executives in this and that kind of position. It is essential to have certain information about each executive individually. What kind of training and experience has he had? How old is he? What kind of ability has he demonstrated? Is he reliable, dependable? Is he capable of assuming greater responsibilities?

The importance of having information which will answer these and other similar questions is quite obvious. Effective planning to utilise present executive resources on future requirements simply cannot take place without it.

Each company should design an Executive Resources Inventory file containing basic information regarding the individual, his education, training and development, experience for executive resources requirements. This must be constantly updated so that the information is adequate and in readily usable form. Two simple tests are suggested for determining whether executive resources inventory is adequate and put up in readily usable form:

- Is it in constant readiness to be taken into a meeting on short notice?
- Will it quickly provide the pertinent information needed to make personnel decisions objectively with respect to filling vacancies, recruitment needs, development programmes, etc.?

Development of Executive Resource Inventory: The approach consists of:

- Establishing and maintaining an inventory of present executive resources.
- Setting up and maintaining a separate record of employees considered immediately qualified for promotion.

### Executive Resources Forecasting

Once we know 'what we do have' the next step is 'what we do need' taking into consideration our future growth plans. Forecasting executive resources requirements is the means of gaining the necessary time to meet future requirements in the most effective manner possible. The dependence of advance planning and preparation on forecast information raises two issues: What kind of information is needed? How can it be developed?

**The kinds of information needed.** Forecasting executive resource requirements is essentially nothing more than trying to determine in advance what kind of executive employment requisitions to expect in the future. How many can be expected from the various parts of the organisations? In what lines of work? When? If the problem is visualised in this manner, the specific type of information which should go into the forecast for each part of the organisation can be readily determined.

**How it can be developed.** Forecasting, if it is to be done satisfactorily, must be approached in an objective manner. The problem of developing forecast information is primarily one of seeking out and systematically utilising information which will most reliably indicate future needs.

Future executive resource needs can be expected to reflect:

- Loss of present executive resources.
- Expansion or contraction in business.
- Growing or declining needs for certain types of executives.

In the first instance, the resulting need will be for replacements. In the latter two, the resulting need will be for more or fewer executives, depending on the nature of the development or the direction of the trend. What kind of information is available in each of these areas which can be used in forecasting what future executive resource requirements will be?

For the purpose of forecasting replacement needs:

- An analysis of future separations under the retirement programme will provide one source of definite and reliable information.
- Early retirements, disability or otherwise, can frequently be determined in advance with reasonable accuracy. These can be reflected in the forecast.
- An anlysis of past experience will provide a basis for projecting future loss through other types of separations such as resignation, involuntary quits, dismissals, etc.

To summarise:

1. Determine the number of replacements.
2. Adjust this figure up and down in light of:
   - expansion or contraction requirements,
   - growing or declining requirements for certain types of executives,
   - any long-term trends which should be reflected.

Project executive requirements sufficiently ahead to allow the necessary time to get ready to meet them. In actual practice this may mean anywhere from two to five or more years, depending on the nature of the requirements.

**The use of forecast and inventory information.** Forecast and inventory information is one of top management's most useful of human resources management tools. It is especially useful in such fundamental areas as:

(a) Planning and making personnel moves — promotion, transfers, demotions, lay-offs etc.

(b) Determining recruitment needs.

(c) Determining training and development needs.

(d) Ensuring management of the services of the best qualified executives and potential executives available.

(e) Ensuring consideration to all qualified candidates on an equitable basis.

(f) Planning changes in organisational structure.

Besides these obvious applications and uses, there are other very substantial benefits to be derived from its development and use. For example, it will stimulate more effective personnel communications. It will serve to get attention focussed in the right direction, by getting executives thinking in terms of performance, abilities, capacities, potential etc. It will cause executives up and down the line to get better acquainted with their immediate subordinates and other employees. These benefits should not only make for a more constructive approach to dealing with the problems directly involved in meeting future executive requirements, but they should also have definite carry-over value in dealing with executive resources, problems in general.

### Executive Resource Individual Development Plan (ERIDP)

The next basic phase in executive resource planning is to get down to the specifics from general executive resource planning to individual career development plan, which would be essential for effective E.D. effort. Determine career paths or development plans for every individual executive, because an individual executive when he joins a company expects a certain career within the company and it follows that the company should develop a career plan for the next immediate period of a year or two, then extend it to long term of 4 or 5 or even 10 years as some organisations do. ERIDP is designed to provide a record of current job assignments and performance, a projection of near and long-term potential and the development needs of the individual. It will be reviewed and revised periodically and shall be available for review by the management. The steps involved are:

- What is the current position responsibilities, along with the month and year assigned to the current position?
- What is overall current performance appraisal?
- What is his promotability? Be specific. List positions to which you feel that the individual is promotable either now or within two-three years.
- What is his possible ultimate potential?
- Why do you say so and on what basis?
- What are his development needs?
- What is your development plan?
- The ERIDP must be prepared and reviewed by the principal line and staff executive and dated.

### Management Succession System (MSS)

MSS is the next important phase in the executive-resource planning relevant and significant in the EDS. MSS should be worked out in the case of every executive position on an executive resource replacement table or a Management Succession Chart.

- Determine the current executive position and incumbent.
- Determine the age and date of appointment on the current appointment.
- Establish the date due for replacement.
- Determine the next appointment to which the incumbent could be promoted (unless he is retiring or quitting the company).
- Is the incumbent ready for promotion? If not, what further training or development or experience is required?
- Identify the possible successors or replacements? Immediate and long-term.
- Determine the successor's or replacement's current position, responsibilities and capacities.
- Determine what further training or development or education or experience is required to fit successor for promotion.
- Determine the date when the successor would be ready for promotion or succession and match this date with the date due for replacement of the incumbent.

## Appendage

The contributions of different factors of production individually and collectively can be measured by the formulae given below:

### (A) Labour

| | | |
|---|---|---|
| Value added per person per employee | (Rs.) | $\frac{\text{Value added per annum}}{\text{Total no. of employees}}$ |
| Manpower productivity | (Rs.) | $\frac{\text{Output of goods \& services}}{\text{Total persons employed}}$ |
| Labour productivity | (Rs.) | $\frac{\text{Production value}}{\text{No. of man hours spent}}$ |
| Worker performance | Ratio | $\frac{\text{Standard time needed for the total work done in a yr.}}{\text{Actual time taken for doing the work during the yr.}}$ |
| Machine performance | % | $\frac{\text{Total standard machine time for work done during the yr.}}{\text{Actual machine time to do the work during the yr.}}$ |
| Machine productivity | (Rs.) per hr. | $\frac{\text{Output of goods \& services}}{\text{Machine hrs. used}}$ |

| | | (B) Capital |
|---|---|---|
| Labour profit productivity | Ratio | $\frac{\text{Profit}}{\text{Wages paid}}$ |
| Return on investment | % | % Margin × Capital turnover |
| Percentage margin | % | $\frac{\text{Gross profit before tax}}{\text{Production value}} \times 100$ |
| Capital turnover | Ratio | $\frac{\text{Production value}}{\text{Investment}}$ |
| | | **(C) Material** |
| Material productivity | Ratio | $\frac{\text{Output of goods \& services per annum}}{\text{Value of material used per annum}}$ |
| Material utilisation | Ratio | $\frac{\text{Materials usefully utilized}}{\text{Total material used}}$ |
| Inventory turnover | Ratio | $\frac{\text{Sale value per annum}}{\text{Average inventory value}}$ |

Contd...

| | | (D) Energy |
|---|---|---|
| Useful energy utilisation | % | $\frac{\text{Total energy used}}{\text{Total energy purchased}} \times 100$ |
| Energy productivity | Rs. | $\frac{\text{Production value of goods \& services}}{\text{Cost of energy dissipated}}$ |
| | | **(E) Overall** |
| Overall productivity | Ratio | $\frac{\text{Total output of all goods \& services}}{\text{Total input cost of all products}}$ |
| Capacity utilisation | % | $\frac{\text{Operating capacity}}{\text{Installed capacity}} \times 100$ |
| Productivity | Ratio | $\frac{\text{Value added}}{\text{Conversion cost}}$ |

Value added is generally taken as value of output of goods and services less value of purchases less excise duty.
Conversion cost is generally taken as labour cost plus equipment cost plus overhead cost.

# Human Resource Development and Management of Stress

7

At the practical level, 'Management' is guided by prioritising problems, a sense of proportion, e.g., balancing apparently contradictory and polar-opposite approaches to issues and trying to find out the optimum middle path in an open and flexible way (as against getting stuck in a fixed perspective) and other situational variables. Management finally happens only through the cycle of growing experience. In fact, integration is nothing more than another name for health and wholesomeness.

Again at a practical level, Human Resource Development is linked with development of our personality, with learning, with satisfaction, with happiness, with love, with freedom, with truth, with balance, fearlessness, wholesomeness and ease in a way to which people can easily relate. Out of it, we have to spin health, pleasure, money, content, respect, development and progress in marital, domestic, occupational, financial, social spheres and so on. There is something in all of us (Nature) that seeks the spiritual and so, healing becomes possible. Today, yoga, meditation, concentration, transcending the mind and its divisive tendencies, reconnecting with one's real self, spiritual growth practices and other stress management techniques have become important components of HRD.

## HRD and Management of Stress

No ordinary mortal can be free from stress. In fact, a lot of industrial problems can be traced to the stress factors like indiscipline, absenteeism, alcoholism, etc., HRD divisions can play an important role in ameliorating, eliminating or changing the stress producing factors, both individual and organizational in the following ways:

(i) Spread information on how to face stress. This may include latest knowledge about stress responses, diet, exercise, music, relaxation methods, meditation etc., which acts as stress safety valves. The family is for many a stress safety valves. Similarly, following the routine way of doing a job is a way of coping with stress.

(ii) Help individuals to find out strategies to alleviate stress.

(iii) Conduct stress audit. Data may be collected with the aid of questionnaires, interviews, physical examination for three types of variables, viz., causal, meditating and end-result. Causal variables are the stressors themselves. Meditating variables are the individuals' personality, culture and non-work environment. End-results are the stress reactions of consequences.

(iv) Pay particular attention to the selection of individuals for inherently stressful situation.

(v) Design organization in such a way that role problems are minimized.

It is important to identify stress and cope with it in a constructive manner. However, stress intensity of a long duration must be avoided. Playing it cool and sense of humour are the popular notions of overcoming stress. The truth is that very often we do have a choice. A person experiencing stress may either accept the problem in a functional way (i.e. accept the challenge in a preferred state called 'Alpha' characterized by calmness) or avoid it in dysfunctional way (in an unpreferred state called 'Non-alpha'). Through practice, observation and patience it is possible to remain in an 'Alpha' state.

*Bhagavad Gita* provides us an insight into the philosophy of stress management in the following lines. A true yogic attitude is to be able to accept everything that comes from the Divine and let it goes easily and without regret.... Yoga becomes the destroyer of sorrows and miseries for him who is moderate in eating, pleasures, work, sleep and other daily affairs.... Fear, anger, anxiety, overwhelming emotions and other negative emotions must be controlled, thereby avoid damage to others and to oneself.... A glorious failure leads to nothing; a petty success may lead to a success that is not petty.... Thy right is to action only, not to the fruits thereof.... Rise again, allow for failures.... Discover the progressive unfolding of your unmanifest potential and the evolution of your immortal soul....

In one of our old Sanskrit books there is a verse which can be translated as follows:

> 'For the family sacrifice the individual, for the community the family, for the country the community, and for the soul the whole world.' What the soul is, few of us can know or tell and each one of us can interpret it in a different way. But the lesson this Sanskrit verse teaches us is the same lesson of harmony, co-operation and sacrifice for the larger good. And to those who are fortunate comes the joy of sacrifice also.

It is difficult to trace a human 'complete' in all respects. Happiness and satisfaction are relative terms. The problem of human happiness is the problem of excessive desires. Human desires are insatiable like our desire for wealth, many possessions, honour, and power, the desire to be loved and thought well off. The wise thing would be to limit desires.

In human nature, unsatisfied needs produce tension. Needs also give rise to conscious action. Needs create tensions—mental strain, nervous anxiety, muscular contraction, physiological stretching, cultural stress, chemical changes, social disequilibrium and these tensions can not be released till some wants are satisfied.

Among the fundamental causes which lead to accident, Human nature and his surrounding atmosphere plays a vital part in this direction. No ordinary mortal can be free from stress and at any given time a person is likely under a number of stresses which may vary in their nature (Financial, Occupational, Domestic, Marital, Social and so on), Intensity (moderate, severe or mild) and duration (acute or chronic). The 'stress tolerance' level varies from person to person (coping ability).

In fact, a lot of industrial problems including accidents, unrest, violence, alcoholism, absenteeism, indiscipline etc., can be traced to the 'stress factor'. Prolonged exposure to stress does generate negative emotions like anxiety, fear, anger etc. Fear may be the cause of many diseases and anger is likely to generate a chain reaction of bad manners and ugly scenes. Among these emotions, anxiety alone can be beneficial if the person is practical (not overreacting), realistic, cool and optimistic.

However, the fact is that stress has to be perceived as positive force. Stress within reasonable limits is not only beneficial but also essential to cope with the problems of living. It helps to clarify one's perception of the problems at hand, to accept the challenge with self-confidence and adopt innovative approaches, in solving the problem.

In fact, every person has got his own limitation of tolerance but it is very important to cope with stress in a constructive manner or at least not be overwhelmed by it. The truth is that we do have a choice often but due to lack of knowledge we may not be aware of the horizons and options. In stress situation, clear logical thinking unhampered by emotions should enable one to evaluate the pros and cons.

The Human Resource philosophy will realize that an individual work performance is a result of two factors, namely: (1) Ability, (2) Attitude. It is the synergistic combination of these two forces together in balance which will result in desired performance. Any of the variables acting in isolation will fail to achieve the desired result. Let us have an Indian Socio-cultural Ethos in all our HRD efforts, i.e. 'YOGAH KARMASU KAUSHALAM' meaning skill in action is yoga.

# Training and Development

# 8

The Human Resource Development philosophy revolves around aspects of 'Training' and 'Development'. Training concentrates on the improvement of interpersonal skills (how to relate satisfactorily to others), decision making skills (how to arrive at the most satisfactory course of action), operative skills (the basic skills related to the successful completion of a task), or a combination of these. A conservative manager may question the desirability of any systematic training programme itself. 'Why should I bother about all these useless details when I can just train up when and under whom I feel absolutely necessary, according to the vacancies created or according to the requirements of the law or Apprenticeship Regulations of the Government?' His attitude may be just 'well, we managed in the past without a training programme, and we will manage in future'.

Training is intimately connected with all the personnel or managerial activities. Training is essential to improve organisational climate, to help a company fulfil its future personnel needs or existing personnel alterations, to improve productivity, quality and company profits. Training is also essential for personal growth, from the point of view of health, safety, to help prevent industrial accidents as also to prevent obsolescene which may be due to age, temperament, or lack of motivation or the inability of a person to adopt himself to his surroundings or to adopt himself to technological changes, or learn operation of machineries or to assist line management in the conduct of administration and follow up action plans to the maximum possible extent.

William Berliner and William Mcharney say that discovering training needs involves five tasks:

(A) Task Description Analysis:

(i) List the duties and responsibilities or tasks of the job under consideration, using the Job Description as a guide.

(ii) List the standards of work performance on the job.

(B) Determining Training Needs:

(iii) Compare actual performance against the standards.

(iv) Determine what part of the job is giving the person trouble, where is he falling down in his performance.

(v) Determine what kind of training is needed to overcome the specific difficulty or difficulties.

The number of trainees that a company would require may be estimated on the basis of the following formula:

$$I = [(R - S) - X] + W,$$

where 'I' means the number of trainees to be accepted for training. 'R' stands for the required number of persons of the category or job for which the training programme is undertaken, 'S' means the supply of available persons of the specified category, 'X' means the expansion through fresh recruitment of persons having the required skill and experience, and 'W' stands for the wastages of personnel in the category or the job concerned. The wastages, in turn may depend on the natural wastage (e.g., separations due to retirement, death, etc.), the voluntary turnover of personnel (e.g., resignations) and the wastages that occur among the trainees during the period of training itself.

Generally, training courses are typically designed for short-term durations or stated set purposes for employees or supervisors through company-designed training programmes while development implies a broader perspective for executives.

## Development

In analysing the skills of a Manager, Katz speaks of three types: (i) Human, (ii) Technical, (iii) Conceptual.

"The managerial personnel must realise that they will not survive unless they keep pace with modern management education, research theory, principles and practices." As JRD Tata had said, "Trained managers are vital to the economic development of the country.... This business of executive management has been one of the most crucial, essential and, at the same time, one of the most difficult elements in providing continuity and efficient management."

The main objective is to accomplish organisational objectives by co-operative action possibly in the actual job environment by way of developing skills, knowledge and attitudes on the tested principles of learning. Some of the prominent training and development methods with their essential characteristics are being summed up as follows:

| Training & Development Methods | Essential Characteristics |
|---|---|
| (1) Mentoring | (i) The practice of 'mentoring' goes far in helping the trainees and fresh recruits settle in with minimum teething pain.<br>(ii) As mentor, it is the senior's responsibility to maintain close contact with his protege and provide the kind of support that will be required—being a philosopher, friend, guide, counsellor, teacher and often enough, as agony uncle/aunt.<br>(iii) Mentoring also helps develop in the senior, a sense of responsibility in the organisation building process and makes him a competent manager or supervisor. |
| (2) On-the-job-training | (i) This method is the most common in training employees in the skills essential for acceptable job performance.<br>(ii) On-the-job-training is also widely used and accepted method of training Executives. |
| (3) Coaching | (i) Coaching will work well if the coach provides a good model with whom the trainee can identify and both can be open with each other.<br>(ii) If the coach accepts his responsibility fully.<br>(iii) If the coach provides the trainee with recognition of his improvements and suitable rewards. |
| (4) Lectures | (i) A lecture can be made interesting and enlist the active participation of the learners with the aid of guided discussion.<br>(ii) The lecturer should pose leading questions, to which the listeners should provide answers apart from giving out knowledge and information. |
| (5) Simulation | (i) Simulation is a mock-up of realities of actual decision-making on the job.<br>(ii) Simulation duplicates the actual conditions encountered on a job.<br>(iii) Very often the participants act differently in real life situations when they do in acting out a simulated exercise. |

| Training & Development Methods | Essential Characteristics |
|---|---|
| (6) Role-playing | (i) Role-playing actually is a method of human interaction which involves realistic behaviour in the imaginary situations. |
| | (ii) The idea of role-playing involves action, doing and practices. |
| | (iii) Role-playing soon demonstrates the gap between thinking and doing. |
| (7) Case study | (i) The case study is based upon the belief that managerial competence can best be attained through the study, contemplation and discussion of concrete cases. |
| | (ii) The trainees are asked to appraise and analyse the problem-situation and suggest solutions. |
| (8) Business or Management Games | (i) It is good technique for developing problem solving and leadership skills. |
| | (ii) On the whole, the trainees almost always react favourably to a well-run game. |
| (9) O.D. | (i) O.D. is a systematic way of introducing change. |
| | (ii) Emphasis on confronting and resolving conflict as a prerequisite to valid problem solving. |
| | (iii) Employing a variety of techniques of self learing and organisational study to bring about the necessary change. |
| (10) T-Group training or sensitivity training | (i) T-group or sensitivity training is a group experience designed to provide maximum possible opportunity for the individuals to develop awareness of self and of others. |
| | (ii) For the individuals to expose their behaviour and experiment with new behaviour. |
| | (iii) For the individuals to give and receive feedback. |
| | (iv) Helps trainees to improve in quality and participation in human affairs. |
| (11) Job Rotation | (i) Job rotation is often designed for beginning level managers. |
| | (ii) Planned progression is more likely to occur at higher managerial levels. |
| (12) Incident method | (i) The members working along for couple of minutes studies written incidents. |
| | (ii) Each member asks himself; what seems to be going on in this incident? What lead can I find here toward facts of the case and issues that stirred people up? |

| Training & Development Methods | Essential Characteristics |
|---|---|
| | (iii) Appended to each incident is an invitation to make short-term decisions in the role of a person who had to cope with the incident when it actually happened. |
| (13) Conference method | (i) The conference method encourages members to express themselves and without forcing agreement, ensure a general consensus. |
| | (ii) The members express their feelings without fear to censure or ridicule, control the more verbose member and bring out the reserved members develop to the thoughts and feelings of others. |
| | (iii) Good and stimulating leaders are needed for it is they who summarise material at appropriate times during a discussion and think along with the group to help it analyse and reach decisions. |
| (14) Programmed instructions | (i) There is a high level of learner motivation in programmed instructions. |
| | (ii) It incorporates a planned course of proceedings pertaining to the learning or acquisition of general knowledge or some specific skills. |
| | (iii) However the cost of creating any such programme is quite substantial. |

## Significance

The significance of training and management development in an organization cannot be overstated. Training of operatives and other employees goes a long way to raise the level of productivity in an organization, by improving their skill and know-how. Particularly in a world of rapid changes in technology and operational approaches, the training in new ways of doing things becomes imperative for doing them in a better way to produce more. When the more progressive concerns in an industry adopt new techniques for raising their level of operational effectiveness, those who would stick to the 'status quo' must lag behind. Training is thus a must for preventing obsolescence.

What is stated above in regard to training of non-executive employees also holds good for management development. In addition to these, in view of the great problems of human relations, both within a group, between the groups and also in respect of relations with subordinates, equals as well as superiors, which senior and middle-level executives (both managerial and non-managerial) face today, acquisition and development of skills in dealing with others assume special significance. Besides, particularly in a developing country like India where the business management so far mainly grew along traditional channels, the importance of professional management is growing day by day, due to the operational effectiveness as well as the legal and environmental compulsions. This naturally underlines the need for developing the professional skills and knowledge of these mangers who did not have the benefit of formal education in management.

### Objectives

From what we have just now stated, it is easy to derive some of the objectives which guide the training and management development programmes at the company level.

### Learning New Techniques

Many programmes aim wholly or partly at helping the employees and managers to acquire new techniques or skills relevant for doing their own works in a better way. This is particularly very important for middle-aged or relatively older persons, for keeping them up-to-date in 'know-how'. Even for the younger people, this is important for acquainting them with a wider background of knowledge and skill, other than what they already possess.

### Induction

However, skilled a worker or manager may be in his own area, due to difference in details of operation and 'culture' in every organization, every new employee has to be trained about the special features, requirements and environment of his work in the new organization.

### The Remedial Measures

Training and management development programmes in many organizations also aim at correcting deficiencies of the employed personnel through appropriate programmes for remedial actions. These often prove very much helpful in raising the level of morale and efficiency of the deficient workers, provided they are organized with tact and understanding, without damaging the self-esteem of the persons concerned.

### Helping Transfers and Promotions

Training and orientation are often required to help the employees taking new positions by transfers or promotions. Depending on the nature of the job and the background of the person concerned, the programme may be short or elaborate.

### Aiding Displaced Employees

In a dynamic business and industrial setting, certain jobs or functions lose their relevance. Sometimes for technological or market factors, the level of activity has to be brought down in a planned manner in certain areas. All these may necessitate displacement of men who, if properly trained or oriented, may be usefully absorbed in other lines of activities in the same organization. Sometimes training emphasis is focussed on these employees.

### Preconditions of Success of Training and Management Development Programmes

As we have already mentioned, many industrial and business organizations in India have commenced training and management development activities of some form or other. These are undertaken in addition to the Apprenticeship Training which, under the Apprenticeship Act, 1961, every industrial establishment in selected industries is required to undertake.

The first prerequisite for the success of training and management development in any organization is the management's active interest and support for these activities. In India, the top management in many organizations look to training as a low priority and dispensable item. This must change.

Another most important preconditions, which is not fulfilled in many organizations in India, is systematic identification of training and management development needs. For this, the three-tier approach recommended by McGehee and Thayer may be useful.

A third important precondition for the success of training and management development programmes in any organization is the provision of adequate finance for these activities in its budget. In this respect also, the situation in India is not encouraging. As one observer reports, 'Even today, when training is being given such an emphasis and is regarded as an essential element of organizational growth, several organizations do not provide adequate funds for training. In other words, the training budget does not form a distinct part of the company's total budget and is clubbed with the budget of some other activity.

In addition to these, it is essential that the trainers for the training programme should be correctly selected. Anyone cannot be a good trainer. He should not only know the subject thoroughly and should have some experience in handling the training-area, but must also be deeply interested in training. He should also have adequate skill in training and should be given proper guidance about its methodology. This last requirement is particularly important for the line-supervisors and functional managers. The Training Manager should help them in this respect and short courses may be offered to them in the particular training methodology which is considered appropriate for their topics.

And last, but not the least, the Training Manager and trainers, before starting any programme, must give ample thought and consideration to the choice of appropriate techniques for training. For this, due attention is to be given to the nature of the training programme, the subject or subjects to be covered, the nature and the level of trainers and the objectives of the particular programme. In industry or business, no single training method can be considered as appropriate in all cases. A proper mix of the training techniques is to be chosen before the commencement of each programme.

## Techniques of Training

In modern industrial and business organizations different methods are used for purposes of training. As we have mentioned above, the selection of the right type of training techniques would depend on the consideration of various factors and may vary from organization to organization. In the following paragraphs we would consider some of the principal methods of training the operatives and non-managerial employees.

## On-the-job-training

The importance of practical on-the-job-training is really great, both for the raw and uninitiated and also for those with some formal education in the technology of the particular work-process. Even for technical education, there being greater emphasis on the theoretical knowledge and general application of that in the work-process, such knowledge has to be supplemented by practical training under the actual work environment and plant conditions in a modern organization. The on-the-job-training, which is usually imparted by the supervisor or a senior employee, actually achieves this. Even for the experienced workers with practical experience in other factories, a brief exposure to the specialities of the machinery and the technology in the particular organization would be helpful, since most organizations have their distinctive technological differences.

### Class-room Instruction

Although presently there is much emphasis upon on-the-job-training and training with the help of teaching-aids, etc., the need of class-room lectures by instructors is still considered unassailable. Particularly in imparting theoretical training or while providing some knowledge input, it is difficult to avoid class-room instruction. However, in the training of mechanical skills, where the significance of muscle coordination and actual performance of work is the greatest, the relative significance of class-room instruction is less. In other jobs as well, the instruction in the class-room should not be entirely lecture-based, but should depend on a suitable mix of lectures and trainer-trainee discussion.

### Apprenticeship Training

In the organizations where skilled operatives are employed in fairly large numbers, formal apprenticeship programmes are conducted. These programmes combine on-the-job-training by the skilled workers with some amount of class-room instruction, providing the basic knowledge and background for the trade or the operation concerned. Under the Apprenticeship Act, 1961, employers in specified industries operating in India are obliged to train a certain number of workers in 'designated' trades according to prescribed national standards. The proportion of the apprentices to workers varies from trade to trade.

### Vestibule Training

This is another training technique in which there is an integration of on-the-job and off-the-job-training. In this kind of training, the trainees are not given instruction to handle the machinery and equipments which are actually used in production, but are given the machines, etc., which are the same as or almost similar to those used in production. The trainees under vestibule training are given instructions on the operation of the machinery in an area, separate from the production department. This method is desirable where the job is difficult, or the machinery to be used are very costly and may be damaged by novices while learning to handle them.

### 'Cooperative' or 'Collaborative' Training

In this type of training also, there is a combination of theoretical class-room instruction with the practical on-the-job-training. Here the theoretical training is provided by the educational institutions, while the practical work-exposure is obtained through part-time or seasonal on-the-job-training in business or industrial organizations. The training which is received by the engineering students in industry at the end of their college education, but before they obtain their degrees, or the training which the students of management institutes receive for two or three months during the vacation after their first year classes, may be cited as illustrations of collaborative or co-operative training.

### New Technologies of Training

In recent years, many new training-aids have been used, particularly in the in-company training programmes of large and prosperous organizations. Film-strips, projectors, computers and, in western countries, even closed-circuit TV are being used for the purposes of training. These audio-visual aids are adding a new dimension to the training methodology and are found to be highly useful in building up the interests of the trainees. However, for most of the Indian organizations many of them are too costly. Moreover, they should be used mainly to supplement and not to supplant the formal training by instructors. No mechanical aid as yet can substitute the direct interaction between the trainer and trainee in clarifying the doubts and difficulties of the trainees during the. process of learning.

### Programmed Learning

Under this new method, the trainees are given specially prepared programmed text-materials. Here the trainee is required to answer specific questions either by writing them in a response-frame or by pushing a button on a machine, immediately after each segment of new information is provided through the programmed material. In the case of a correct answer, he is allowed to move on to the next step or segment of information. If the answer is wrong, the trainee is immediately given an indication of his mistake and is referred to a branch-programme in which he has to try again, or to attempt another approach. The method has been found to be highly useful in training involving factual materials, or pieces of information. But it may not be of much use in the training courses which provide particular skills, or aim at changing attitudes.

### Methods of Development of Managers

The skill in management, in addition to the knowledge of the relevant matters and practice of the art of management, depends a good deal on the growth of the appropriate attitudes and behavioural styles in the manager concerned. The training of managers thus encompasses several approaches and techniques to develop these appropriate attitudes, besides the instructions in the relevant areas of knowledge and practices of management. It is mainly for this reason that the term 'development' is more frequently used instead of 'training', while referring to the managers. In the following paragraphs we discuss some of the principal methods of development of managers.

### On-the-job-training

As management is essentially an art, where 'how to do' is an essential element of development of managers, to enable them to pick up the details of the appropriate practices in their particular areas of management, they are trained in the 'art of doing' through actual assignments in the relevant managerial functions. However, such training in actual practice should not be unplanned and haphazard. They must be properly planned by the head of the department or divisions, or for top-level managers by a director or the Managings Director himself. Special attention is to be given to the particular assignments meant for the manager, which would be helpful for his future responsibilities or positions. He is also to be properly guided in his work and for that his immediate boss or some other manager has to be given special responsibility. There should be an adequate arrangement for evaluating his performance in these on-the-job activities and recording its results in a proper way. 'Coaching' and 'Understudy assignments' are two usual techniques used to develop the managers or executives in their on-the-job-training. In the case of 'coaching', a senior manager who is entrusted with the responsibility of training a junior manager actually observes the latter while at work. If he makes a mistake, he is corrected and shown the right way of doing it. The role of the manager-coach here is almost the same as that of an athlete-coach.

In the case of understudy assignments, a junior staff-assistant or executive is assigned to a senior executive with the specific responsibility to relieve the latter of some of his works, which he may assign to the former. While the understudy assistant or the executive does the specific works assigned to him, he is also given due encouragement and guidance to learn them. The method is very useful in helping an executive to learn the details of a job. However, if the superior does not have the proper attitude or willingness to instruct his understudy in the art of management, the learning naturally would suffer.

### Job-Rotation

Under this method a manager or executive, who is being considered for promotion with higher and wider responsibilities, is given different types of job assignments to enable him to learn and understand their operations well. In career planning, this is widely used for broadening or developing the managers who are being considered as potential successors to higher positions.

### Company Training Courses

Sometimes these are also described as 'In-Company Training Programmes'. Under these programmes an organization sponsors and conducts formal training courses in general management, or in specific areas of management. The trainees or participants are all selected from the organisations, own executives, or managers who are required to attend the course on a full-time basis. During the days of training they are relieved of their routine responsibilities. The faculty are drawn mainly from the senior managers or executives of the particular funtional areas in which the training is offered. In addition to the internal faculty, external faculty are also brought in from management institutes, universities, professional associations and, in a few cases, from some other leading organizations as well. The main advantage of these courses lies in the fact that they are tailored to suit the goals and requirements of the organizations concerned. However, as the trainees are all drawn from the same company, there may be some narrowness in interests and these programmes usually cannot have the benefit of mutual interaction of the experienced managers of different organizations, which is possible in general training programmes open to all intending organizations. These programmes mainly rely on lectures, class-room discussions, group discussions and case-studies of specific management problems.

### Management Development Programmes Organized by Management Institutes, etc.

Now-a-days, different management institutes, research institutes and also some professional bodies offer Management Development Programmes in specific functional areas of management, as well as in general management. These programmes are announced in newspapers well in advance and brochures containing the courses offered and other relevant particulars are sent to the industrial or business organizations. The courses usually are of short duration (usually from 3 days to 14 days) and mostly are residential in nature, i.e., the participant trainees are required to stay together. Now-a-days, some programmes accept a few non-residential participants as well. Those programmes continue for the whole days during their duration and the participants nominated by different organizations are deputed on duty-leave to attend the courses. These courses make use of varied techniques, e.g., lectures, group discussions, role-playing, educational visits, problem-solving exercises, case-studies, experience-sharing by participants, etc. The faculty is mainly drawn from the sponsoring institute or the association and is supplemented by guest speakers from the leading business or industrial organizations who present their own experiences in the specific functional areas. A great advantage of such courses is a good blend of the theoretical and practical inputs, which are available in these programmes from the experts belonging to the management institutes and the functioning executives who attend them, either as trainees or guest faculty. The mutual interactions between the functioning executives from different organizations who stay together and also share the same training sessions facilitate the processes of training and understanding to a great extent.

### Seminars and Conferences

Sometimes top-level managerial personnel are invited to attend seminars or conferences on specific management problems or areas.

Usually these are sponsored by professional bodies, or research or management institutes. The sponsors prepare some theme papers which are distributed among the participants.

The sessions on each subject commence with a lecture presentation by an expert, selected by the sponsoring organization. These lectures and theme papers raise specific issues for consideration by the participants who hold thorough discussions on them, on the basis of inputs provided by the participants and also by the theme papers. The educative values of these seminars are immense, as the participants are made aware of many new ideas, problems and techniques in their own functional areas and may discuss them at the professional level with the top experts on the subject. However, these cannot be used with so much success for the development of young or junior executives, unless they are supplemented by formal training courses.

One variety of these seminars is known as the 'workshop'. In a 'workshop' the participants are given one or more specific problems with some necessary background-inputs, provided through reading materials or lectures. They are then split up into small groups according to the problems, or on the basis of identity of interests. The groups deliberate on the specific problems and work out their practical solutions. A report containing these solutions is then prepared by each group and presented before the General Session, which all participants of the workshop attend. A final report of the workshop is then prepared after considering the reports of different groups.

### Case-studies

As there is not much scope for trainees in management subjects having off-the-job training to learn through practical experiments, an alternative approach in examining management problems and practices is tried out in the form of 'case-studies'. Under this method one specific problem *or* situation is picked up from the actual experience of working in an organization. This is then recorded in all its details along with the necessary background information and is presented to the participants of a management development course, or in-company programme in the form of cyclostyled hand-outs for detailed analysis. Each trainee is required to study the case and work out his own approach or solution for the problem. These are then presented before the class and the best possible solution is worked out through discussions in which all trainees and instructor participate.

In some case-studies, the actual solution that was tried out in the particular organization is also presented. This is then considered along with the analysis of the problem and an evaluation is made. If the tried solution is not considered as the best, the alternatives are examined.

In addition to the problem-oriented case, now-a-days case-studies, which just describe interesting management practices in a particular field in an important organization, are also analysed and evaluated in training sessions. Sometimes, two or three; such cases on a single management area in two or three organizations are taken together and compared. Such comparative case-studies are found to be of immense value in understanding the possibilities of different approaches to a single management practice which may be possible under different contexts.

As a method, the case-study is highly useful in understanding or evaluating application of theoretical knowledge inputs in actual practice at the level of an organization. It was first developed and tried out in Harvard Business School and its success there as a pedagogic method helped its spread to all leading management institutes throughout the world. However, if the discussion-leader or the instructor cannot handle the case-discussion in the proper manner, the participants may not feel interested in the case. The method then would fail to serve its purpose.

**Role-playing**

Another method of management instruction is 'Role-Playing' in which a particular management problem-situation is simulated by trainees who assume the roles of managers or employees and outsiders and try to re-create the situation. The trainees behave according to their own ideas, approaches and understanding without any prompting, or advice from anybody else. They try to react to the situation as they would do in a real life case. After the role-playing session is over, the trainees and the instructors sit in a session to discuss the behaviour and actions of the role-players and evaluate them. The mistakes committed are identified and better approaches which could have been tried in that situation are considered. The method is found as a very useful technique in creating and maintaining the interests of the participants in the problem concerned and in working out a solution instantly. However, at times, if not handled with care and seriousness, the role-play may degenerate into a frivolous exercise in which the dramatic aspect may overshadow the learning process.

### Committee Assignments

Now in most of the organizations which are managed in modern and professional ways, several committees of managers function regularly. Although these are almost always appointed for objectives other than that of management development, some of them can be, and are, used for developing managers. Many of these committees are assigned specific responsibilities for decision-making in which managers and heads of different departments share their own views, problems and possibilities relating to the assigned area. The results of their deliberations are presented in the form of recommendations to the managing director for his consideration or for consideration by the Board, if necessary. These deliberations help the managers examine specific issues from a wider standpoint, broader than the narrow angle of their own specific departments or functional areas. In some organizations, an executive committee, or one or two functional committees consisting of senior managers are appointed to assist the Board of Directors in the solution of the company's problems. The Executive Committee brings to the Board the point of view of the professional managers who are directly connected with these problems. They also collect and consider all the relevant data and provide the Board with the complete set of background materials, along with their summaries and recommendations for quick decision-making. Naturally this saves much of the time of the Directors of the Board and also helps them to get all relevant details ready at hand.

### Management Games

The management game is one of the simulation techniques used in management development. In these games, there are several 'teams' each of which acts as a 'firm' (or, in specific cases, as an 'interest group') to operate for certain objectives in a specific 'period'. These teams compete or interact with one another in the presence of 'observers' who include the instructors and some of the participants. The gains and losses of each team are calculated in rounds and at the end of the period the 'winner' is chosen. The games are followed by post-mortem sessions, in which the observers and participants analyse the behaviour and mistakes of the teams and general lessons are drawn.

### Sensitivity Training

This off-the-job training technique is also known as 'T-group training' or 'laboratory training'. It mainly deals with developing or changing the attitudes or behavioural patterns of the trainees. In these training sessions, the participants discuss their real problems, learn more about themselves, particularly their weaknesses and emotions and develop insights into how others react to their behaviour and how they themselves react to others. They try to sort out inter-personal problems. Usually these groups do not have any set agenda and work mainly in an unstructured way. The participants learn mainly by analyzing and understanding one's own or other's emotions and also through mutual interactions.

Supporters of sensitivity training claim great success in improving the behaviour and attitudes of the managers through this technique. The critiques, on the other hand, are equally emphatic about its dangers and limitations. They maintain that in several cases the sensitivity training sessions have caused tremendous emotional problems for individual participants. In some cases, inter-personal relations between the peers, or between supervisors and subordinates, have been more embittered following the in-company sensitivity training sessions. However, in spite of the controversy, it has to be accepted that this method is a very interesting technique for attempting a change in the behavioural patterns, although it must be handled carefully and be guided only by experts trained in this.

### Organizational Development

Under the techniques of development of managers which we have discussed so far, the emphasis is on the development of individuals holding managerial or senior executive positions. In recent years, another approach, Organizational Development (OD) aimed at changing the 'values' and 'culture' of the entire organization in addition to changing the individual managers has been in vogue. Organizational Development emphasizes the necessary changes in inter-personal and inter-group relations for the purpose of bringing the necessary changes in the behavioural pattern and culture in the organization to make it more conducive to the growth of the individual managers. Its main characteristic is that it encompasses the entire organization, instead of individuals. Some of the techniques which are used in OD are identical with specific techniques of manager-development. T-group sessions, for example, are common to both. However, T-groups in OD are used more as one of the steps in an integrated programme involving all or several working groups of an organization; while 'T-group' sessions in a manager-development programme covers only a selected group of trainees whose training period is identical.

Another important technique of OD is known as "Management Grid". In this technique, a series of questionnaire and simulation exercises are used to force the managers to face and realize the gap between their ideal and actual behaviour. Once the gap is recognized, the managers are expected to initiate necessary changes in themselves and in their work-environment on their own, or at least to accept attempts to such changes.

Confrontation is another well-known technique of organisation development. Under this technique, a group is confronted with feedbacks on their current performance, so as to make them unhappy about their own shortcomings. Such feedbacks may originate from 'T-group' sessions in which managers meet their own peers or subordinates. Sometimes, inter-group meetings of managers who are functionally interdependent on each other, or TV or tape-recorded playbacks of ordinary management meetings can generate feedbacks for identification of weak spots. Management games also have been used as a technique of confrontation in some cases.

Employees' Attitude Surveys have also been used in OD programmes. Similarly, a planned series of meetings between individual managers and their peers or subordinates also have been used for this purpose. All these generate facts and data to identify actual or potential problems about which the managers had been ordinarily unaware.

Sometimes, for improving inter-group relations, the OD consultants arrange for heart-searching by two groups in the organization which had difficulties in working together in the past. Each group first meets alone and considers how it views the other group. What the other group thinks of its feelings about the other, and how does the other group views it (according to its own impressions). The two groups then meet together and share the lists of questions and answers with the other. Arguments are not permitted, although any group can ask for elaboration or enlargement of its answers. These sessions help in clearing up misunderstandings in certain cases and, in others, at least help in providing sufficient insight on the inter-group relations and problems.

In recent years, OD has spread well as a management development and problem-solving approach and naturally has been helpful, in many cases, in identifying the sources of inter-group problems and facilitating the adoption of corrective steps. However, it would be wrong to exaggerate its effectiveness. It may help in improving the climate in an organization, to the extent to which it was influenced by problems connected with inter-personal relations, personal sensitivity, or group psychology. However, there are many organizational problems which are not behavioural or psychological in nature at all. They may have their origin in economic factors, or social, or political environment. In spite of better understanding of inter-personal and inter-group attitudes, the sources of conflict originating from such economic, social or political factors cannot be removed by OD. They require specific remedies for specific maladies. For example, where the problems originate from inadequacies of rewards or from the defective workflows, or job-assignments, remedies such as wage-revisions, incentive-wages, job-enrichment, or reassignment of jobs are indispensable and without them, OD would be useless. It is true that attitude changes attempted through OD may help structural changes, if they go together. But to expect that attitude changes should always come first and that alone can bring structural changes would be too naive. In fact, total improvement in an organization should depend on both types of these changes. OD has importance as an approach to achieve one of them. And that itself is not a small gain.

## Evaluation of the Effectiveness of Training and Management Development

Against the complaint of the training managers regarding the inadequacy of training funds, the top policy-makers in the conservative organizations often reply that the result of training cannot be ascertained, and as such it is worthwhile to spend more money on items which yield immediate and tangible results. In more modern and progressive organizations, however, regular techniques are used to ascertain the effectiveness of training, although not always in quantifiable terms.

### Trainee Feedback

A very simple and inexpensive method of ascertaining the effectiveness of a particular training programme is to get a feedback in prescribed forms, from the trainees who attended it. In these feedback forms they indicate their options about the course-contents, methods of teaching, effectiveness of trainers, the extent to which they have gathered new knowledge or skill and derived benefits from the programme and so on. Although it is good to know about the trainees opinions about the course contents and other things the feedback may show personal bias of the trainees in regard to the individual trainers or specific topics of training. Sometimes, the trainees, for various reasons, may try to be tactful. Hence too much value should not be attached to this instrument, although it is desirable to have some arrangement of trainee-feedback to supplement other instruments of evaluation.

### Pre-training and Post-training Behaviour

A better technique may be the evaluation of the behaviour and performance of the trained executives or other employees by their bosses and peers, before and after training. They are specifically instructed to observe whether there is any definite evidence of improvement in these respects following the training. In some cases, even the subordinates are asked to evaluate the behaviour of the trained executives before and after the training. The last alternative, of course, has a great limitation, as the personal expectations and backlog of relations with the subordinates may considerably affect the objectivity. But comparative evaluation of pre-training and post-training behaviour, in spite of some chance of bias, may be highly useful as they are better acquainted with the objectives, responsibilities, opportunities and constraints, subject to which the trainee has to work.

### Comparison of Trained and Untrained Personnel

Another technique, which may be more free from the bias element, mentioned above, is the comparison of the behaviour and performance of a trained group of executives or employees with those of some other groups doing the same types of jobs, but having no training at all. It is preferable that such evaluation should not be done by the boss alone. He should work in collaboration with some other managers of the same or higher ranks, including at least one representative from the training department or section.

Training and development is structured around 3 Ps, i.e., people-products-profits in the following sequence:

(i) People create the products, markets for the products and the delivery systems that sell the products.

(ii) When the product sells well, profits are generated.

(iii) When profits are reinvested in people and products, more products/markets result creating more profits.

(iv) People also contribute to profits through application of intelligence in improving efficiency, reducing costs and ensuring cost competitiveness.

It is unlikely that the companies which do not have a system of HRD would invest in training and development programmes, identification and determination of training needs and required number of trainees in order to improve productivity, profitability and quality development with regard to future changes and challenges, competitive market situation and other situational variables.

Datta (1991) proposes that for a proper process of integration of the personnel, the training and development efforts of the organisation must aim at (a) creating attitudes and skills of proactive response to future challenges; (b) creating ability to strike an appropriate balance between centralization and decentralization; (c) creating an open outlook to learn from feedback (even from subordinates); (d) creating multidisciplinary teams; and (e) creating a fusion of technologies and humanities.

Training itself needs a shift of focus according to the new developments. The focus would be more on general aptitudes than on specific abilities. Cohen (1991) predicts that 'Training technology will shift from job specifics to individual diagnosis and development.' The traditional evaluation methods that assume prior experience also needs to be changed. Since new technology is characterized by functional flexibility, training should be designed in such a way to develop cross-functional and multi-skilled personnel.

The organization for economic co-operation and Development proposes a solution to this problem in work related training, on-the-job-training, special training provided by new technology suppliers, training organized by firms with the aid of external bodies and vocational training itself (OECD).

# Managing Change

# 9

Culture, as Webster's Dictionary defines it, is "the integrated pattern of human behaviour that includes thought, speech, action and artifacts and depends on man's capacity for learning and transmitting knowledge to succeeding generations."

Change is the law of nature. No individual or organisation can escape change. Change is defined as planned or unplanned alteration of the status quo in an organism situation or process. It affects the structure, technology and human resources of the total organisation.

The areas in which planned change are required include the knowledge change (conceptual understanding of new objects, processes, etc.), the skill change (new ways of doing things through practice), the attitude change (adoption of new feelings); and the value change (adoption of new beliefs, ideas) etc.

Technological change is defined as "the provision of new information or knowledge that is used effectively in industrial operations and has measurable effects on costs, product qualities, level of output or sales, and other ancillary operations of the firm". The definition also includes the provision of new information that affects management and it specifically includes the instruction of the worker on the production floor in the efficient use and operation of existing machinery as well as of new equipment.

Technological changes are basically due to "the search for new markets and business opportunities; development of an in-house technological capability; enhancement of quality for products and services; rationalization and modernization of production facilities; and enhancement of the technical and managerial skills of senior personnel. The expectations underlying all these motivations are that sales will increase along with market share enabling the firm to become more competitive as a result."

## Organisation Change Model

G.L. Lippitt has suggested an organisation change model which is also referred to as "Confrontation model", i.e., appropriate response to the situations that arise in an organisation. This model looks upon an organisation as a living organism and describes the informal and external force influencing it in the growth stages. The principle elements of the model are:

| | |
|---|---|
| Situations | This is the focal point in the model. It includes such terms as "confrontation", "crisis", "problem solving" and "everyday decisions". Thus a strike, financial crisis, accident in factory, change in top leadership are all covered by situations. A situation may not always be a problem. The situations test whether individuals and groups are able to face and meet the challenges. |
| Renewal stimulator | This shows the ability to respond appropriately to the situations. The appropriateness of response will depend upon the adequacy of the action, e.g., whether the action optimized the effective utilization and development of human resources in the organisation, is it responsive to the environment in which organisation exists etc. |
| Human Resources | Individual, pairs, groups and large units of persons in the organisation constitute the human resource. The organisation recognises that technology today is not about tools or machines only but demands the involvement of human resources. The multiple goals of an organisation are achieved through them by human relations. |
| Interfacing | This is the process through which human resources confront common areas of concern, engage in meaningful related dialogues, actively search for |

| | |
|---|---|
| | solutions to mutual problems and purposefully cope with these solutions. |
| Oragnisational Growth | This refers to the concept that organisations are complex organism that have a life cycle with stages of development commencing with birth and progressing through survival to later stages of maturity. In its various stages, this resembles the mental and psychological growth of an individual from boyhood to manhood. |

Human resources are the essential element in the change process. Changes in technology, affect workers by creating gaps in knowledge, values and behaviour and are sometimes resisted. The process of change and growth of an organisation depend upon the situations are handled by the management. This model emphasises 'the need for organisation system to re-examine its goals, evaluate its performance and renew its spirit; and it demonstrates that the ability of the socio-technical system to cope is an essential element'.

So for as managers are concerned, "The shift will be away from traditional skills such as organisation planning, control, follow up and perception. Managers will learn esoteric yet critical skills such as credibility, visioning, ethical judgement, strategic thinking, versatility and courage."

# HRD Climate and OCTAPACE Culture

# 10

HRD climate is an integral part of organisational climate. It can be defined as the employee's perception about the developmental environment of their organisation. This may include a number of characteristics such as the following:

- Importance given to human resources
- Openness of communication
- Encouragement given to risk taking and experimentation
- Feedback given to employees to make them aware of their strengths and weaknesses
- A general climate of trust
- Faith in employee's capabilities
- Employee's tendency to help each other and to collaborate with each other
- Team spirit
- Tendency to discourage stereotypes and favouritism
- Supportive personnel policies and practices.

The essence of HRD climate is the importance which it gives to the development of OCTAPACE culture (developed by T.V. Rao and Udai Pareek) in an organisation. OCTAPACE stands for eight important values viz.,

| *Values* | *Indicators* |
|---|---|
| Openness | Disclosure of one's feelings |
| Confrontation | Facing problems and finding their solutions |
| Trust | Mutual confidence |
| Authenticity | Willingness to acknowledge one's feelings |

| | |
|---|---|
| Proaction | Willingness of the organisation to take initiative in influencing a situation instead of merely reacting to it |
| Autonomy | The quality of an individual to seek help from others without feeling inferior |
| Collaboration | Members working in teams and |
| Experimentation | Taking action on a trial basis initially. |

Organisations differ in the extent to which they possess the above characteristics. OCTAPACE culture is the prerequisite of an effective organisation. In the HRD climate questionnaire (see Appendix), average of all the scores of all the items is taken as the HRD climate. The greater this score the more conducive the organisational climate is for the success of HRD programmes.

T.V. Rao elaborates OCTAPACE culture thus "When people become open in terms expressing their ideas and feelings we can get the best in them. Openness brings new ideas, approaches and skills and talent to the organisation and satisfaction and even a sense of excitement to people. Openness combined with proactivity encourages self-expression and gives rise to discovery of new approaches, methods and competencies. They pave the way for growth.

Collaboration and team-work provide the strength to the organisation to perform. People derive strength from each other through the joy of working together. The WE feeling created serves many purposes. It also gives stamina for people to meet a turbulent environment and solve problems. Confrontation of problems when they arise enhances the problem solving capability of the groups and the organisation.

Trust and authenticity make life enjoyable besides reducing negative emotions and wastage of time of people. When people mean what they say a carry out the promises they make there will be no need for follow up and frustration gets reduced. Human dignity begins to emerge. Trust is a wonderful thing and we can become more trustworthy when we do what we say and we don't say what we cannot do.

Autonomy and experimentation provide opportunities for people create organisational spaces for themselves and make an impact in their own ways in each of the job they perform.

# Building Your Subordinates

# 11

Waiting to develop your subordinates is an admirable goal. Doing something about it is even more admirable. But congratulations alone are not all that is needed. There's still the pay off question: Are the time and efforts you spend on developing subordinates really improve their job performance and their capabilities?

The answer is a vital one. Far from being an extra frill, employee development is at the core of the supervisor's job. The efficiency of his department depends largely on how close his subordinates come to fulfilling their job potentials.

When employee's potential doesn't develop, it may be because the supervisor is misdirecting his efforts. Here are three approaches that can help him zero in on the target of better job performance.

1. Concentrate on the employee's strengths, not his weaknesses. Correcting weaknesses seems like a logical way to develop an employee, yet often it's a waste of time. We might take a tip from the Hollywood producer who is trying to turn an actress into a star. First, he carefully appraises her assets and her shortcomings. He usually finds she has weaknesses of two kinds. Some, like poor diction, can be remedied through training. But others are unalterable and instead of trying to correct them he minimizes them and concentrates on exploiting the girl's good points. If her left profile is poor, he uses camera angles that focus on her right profile. If she gets seasick in a rowboat, he uses a double for those scenes.

The same principle can be applied to developing an employee. Perhaps there are some things he doesn't do well because he lacks experience, training or interest. These deficiencies can be remedied. But there are other things he doesn't do well simply because he has no talent for them.

Instead of hammering at these weaknesses, the superior will get better performance if he concentrates on identifying, promoting and building the employee's strengths. If there's a problem area in an employee's performance, encourage him to find ways of improving it by utilising his strong points.

Here is an example of just such a case. A bright, hard-working employee was an excellent organizer who worked well with people. But, he was a complete flop with any assignment that required careful, methodical, detail work. Every year he went over this shortcoming with his supervisor. Together they worked out increasingly complicated schemes to overcome it. Finally, he agreed to keep track of his time almost hour by hour, making daily, weekly, monthly and quarterly reports of progress in overcoming his weakness. But there was no progress to report. The supervisor realised that the plan for overcoming the employee's inability to do detail work required exactly that kind of work, which he could not do.

The supervisor then decided to attack the problem through the employee's strength — his ability to work with people. The element in his job that required detail work was keeping a personnel record system. Encouraged by his supervisor, he worked out a plan with other employees so that they would do all the detail work necessary.

2. Tie development closely to the employee's daily activities. At General Electric, managers get together once a year with each of their subordinates to draw up a programme of personal development for the year ahead.

Some plans are elaborate, some are simple, but most of them have the subordinate doing something outside of his regular job taking a course serving on a task force, attending professional meetings. These plans are also filled with good resolutions, such as "Remember not to lose temper" or "Plan further ahead".

There is nothing wrong with constructive outside activities and good resolutions and they may produce results. But it's more likely that they will be lost and forgotten under the pressure of the employee's daily work. Since these daily activities absorb most of his attention and energy, here is where you should look for ways in which he can develop.

How to go about it? For a clue, review your own career for a moment. You probably learnt and grew most from doing your work, but your development was not even and continuous. When you started a new job or ran into a fresh problem, you were stimulated to grow rapidly. Then as you got on top of your job and much of it became routine, the growth curve flattened out. Perhaps you began to feel a little stale.

Clearly, then the introduction of new situations and new challenges into a subordinate's job will stimulate his development. Of course, employees cannot always be doing something new; most of their work will have to be familiar. But a new element can be introduced at appropriate intervals, a higher goal, a new task, a new way of doing an old task.

Newness in itself is not enough, however. The new element in the job must perform two functions. It should be something useful to the department and it should make greater demands on the employee's capabilities so that he will have to increase his knowledge and skills in order to accomplish it.

Here is how one supervisor gave a subordinate a new task that filled both these requirements. The employee was a promising young mechanical engineer, but he had only a skimpy knowledge of materials. His supervisor asked him to make a materials study of the product he was working on. This assignment required him to learn more about materials and also to reduce the product's cost by finding less expensive material.

3. Give the employee positive feedback on his performance. Many supervisors spend plenty of time letting their employees know how they are doing and the result is nothing. There is no improvement in the job performance and in some cases the "frank" talk creates resentment.

A common cause of this failure is negative feedback. At General Electric this point is brought home to managers in a "hide and seek" game. A group of 15 or 20 managers sit around a large table. One man is sent out of the room. The rest then hide a small object — let's say a cigarette lighter. They are instructed to help the man find the lighter, but only with negative comments. When he returns he is told — "You are too far away, You are too high, You are on the wrong side of the room". After he has found the lighter, the whole game is repeated but this time he is given only positive feedback: "Go further to the right, Higher, You are very close".

The result of this game seldom varies. With positive feed-back, the seeker finds the object in about half the time that it takes him when he gets only negative hints. And far fewer instructions are needed.

Yet a supervisor's appraisal of his subordinate often is put in negative terms — a list of things he failed to do. "You leave things to the last minute", is a typical remark. The supervisor could just as easily say, "If you make a day-to-day plan and stick to it, you will find you won't have a last minute rush".

A variation of the hide and seek game demonstrates another useful principle for informing employees about their performance. In this game, instructions given to the seeker refer to what he was doing sometime before his last move. For example: "When you first came in the door, you went in the wrong direction". If he can't remember what direction he took, these instructions will confuse rather than help him.

In the same way, if a supervisor saves up his comments for weeks or months, neither he nor the employee will be able to recall clearly what happened and why. To be most effective, comments on an employee's performance should be given as soon as possible, after the specific action.

A second variation of the hide and seek game exposes the futility of another common appraisal technique making comments based on the employee's personality. The man looking for the lighter will be told, "You aren't being aggressive enough in your hunt. You need to show more creativity in finding the lighter". At one such session the seeker finally bursts out, "When are you going to quit kidding around and give me some real help the way you gave the others?"

Most subordinates will justifiably react the same way when they are appraised in terms of their personality defects. They will be more receptive to constructive, specific suggestions on their work than to comment on their personal characteristics. A carefully worked out plan based on these suggestions will help the employee convert them into improved job performance.

Putting these three employee-development principles into effect calls for thought and patience. But they can go a long way towards making your subordinates more effective on their present jobs and developing their potentialities for promotion.

# Human Relations in Organizations

# 12

Between a plan and its actualization is the man more complex than any plan. Without his help, plans cannot be put into actions. If there are distortions or resistances within him, they will reflect themselves to prevent the translation of the most ingenious plan into actual operation. To ignore the human factor, therefore, is to ignore the most important link between the 'input' of resources and the 'output' of wealth.

In this country one observes a lopsided emphasis on the tangible factors of production — on machines, materials and methods. This is not so because the human factor is considered less important. It is because management is not sure whether this factor can be brought within the field of definition, measurement and observable change or control. The fact is, it can be.

The science of human relations in industry concerns itself with problems of organising, controlling, evaluating and developing people so as to draw forth their best in the interest of maximum productivity for the concern and maximum personal satisfaction for the employee.

In our present state of culture, whenever men work together they create relational problems. Within industry, these problems may reveal themselves at any point of human contact. Most frequently that point of contact is where employees meet their immediate superiors. The problem may manifest itself in one to one relationship or between two groups. It may reveal itself as a bid for status or a problem of insubordination. It may take the shape of continuous resistance to change or a sudden slow down of work. It may indicate a blockage in communication or reveal itself in a plethora of complaints and grievances. It may indicate a need for building the general level of motivation or call for a change in basic personnel policies. Whatever shape it may take, it calls for a specialised frame of reference popularly called the human relations approach in industry. Without this frame of reference, no administrator is equipped to manage men. The human relations approach is one about which volumes have been written. To sum it up in a few lines, is to face the danger of giving a lopsided or superficial treatment to the subject. Nevertheless, faced with an option we can only try to do our best in the following few pages.

The human relations approach is based on the fact that an efficient employee is normally the satisfied employee. Satisfaction is a complex phenomenon. It is not merely an outcome of adequate wages because the work situation is not merely a place to earn one's bread. It is a place where the employee gets an opportunity to express himself, an opportunity to participate with others, recognition for what he contributes to the organization and an opportunity for personal growth and development. Expression, participation, recognition and development are as essential to human being as adequate financial returns and proper working conditions.

*Expression* is almost synonymous with living. Man expresses himself in a variety of ways, but the work situation provides the most important channel of expression. Nearly every job and certainly all above the first line supervisory level can therefore be enlarged and made increasingly varied, interesting and challenging. To know the significance of one's job, to have the freedom to communicate and receive communication about it, to suggest changes and see them implemented, etc., satisfies an employee's urge for creative expression to a great extent. Drucker relates the I.B.M. story which shows that even semi-skilled jobs can be "maximised" with an increased variety of functions, made flexible within limits with reference to the work rate and rhythm.

*Participation* means to know what is going on, to have a voice, to be consulted, to belong to a group which asks for and values one's opinions. A decision that is codetermined has far more chances to work out in practice than one that is superimposed upon those who are expected to put it into action. After all, so long as the decision is not actualised, it is really little more than a verbal solution. A solution can be converted into a decision only when people decide to work it out and they can be best motivated to do so if it is their own solution. Participation creates this motivation and lays the basis for effective team-work.

To be recognised for one's worth and receive credit when due, is a deep-rooted urge in all of us. Recognition and credit, however, must be objective. Employees do not want either unjustified criticism or paternalism and they welcome evaluation free from judgmental overtones. Such an evaluation is in the nature of a diagnosis and whether made personally in a one to one relationship or formally launched in the shape of a merit rating programme, helps better performance and gives a measure of security to the employees.

*Growth and development* implies an opportunity to reach somewhere, to receive the necessary assistance and training in order to qualify for jobs needing higher skills and carrying better prospects. A policy of selection from within the concern and training programmes facilitates employee development. This in turn builds up the realisation that the growth of the company is linked with one's individual growth. Team spirit is always fostered where there is an identity of goal. At a higher stage, technical or relational training programmes merge into a personal development programme especially for executives.

The approach embodying expression, participation, recognition and development can be applied for both preventive as well as for curative purposes. It is an approach that prevents relational problems as well as helps resolve them if and when they arise. Obviously its application cannot remove all conflicts or differences of opinions. Certain problems arise not so much from a clash of personalities as from the nature of the situation itself. They reflect, not so much lack of relational skills, as genuine differences in perspectives. These problems reveal the necessity for logical thinking based upon an operational approach.

To put the human relations approach into practice in the everyday administrative work, in conferences with employees and their representatives, in training sessions, whilst introducing technological changes and in fact in any situation where it is needed, calls for human relations skill that does not come easily to the average line manager. This is understandable because both the knowledge and the accompanying skill constitute relatively new fields of research. It is possible that a few wise men throughout history may have understood and applied them; and there are always those rare individuals who have an instinctive understanding of human relations without any formal training. But for most of us they have to be learnt or perhaps rediscovered afresh. There is already a growing body of knowledge gathered ardently and often painfully from laboratories as well as from actual work situations that would help us acquire greater insight and skill regarding problems of human relationship in industry. For instance the application of the non-directive approach to resolving relational problems, the field of group dynamics dealing essentially with problems of changing group attitudes, the new learning theories that facilitate rapid and economical training and the recent findings on communications that help the interviewer, the conference leader, the trainer and the evaluator alike, are there to be applied if line managers are willing to do so.

The scope for applying the human relation approach is greatest in everyday administrative functions of line managers; in matters such as complaints and grievances, in the management of transfers downgrading and discharge, in maintaining discipline, in effecting changes in work assignments, in developing employee services, in planning incentive or merit rating programmes, etc.

In this country, the human relation approach is often dismissed as either long talk or an attempt at mollycoddling. The truth is that the human relation approach has nothing to do with drawing room decorum or paternalism. It does not advocate smooth diplomacy or subtle tricks to get around men; nor, it is an attempt to get at the hidden psychological weakness of employees in order to exploit their weaknesses. It is an approach that accepts an individual in his own right; that seeks to create a psychological climate of permissiveness and positive regard for employees. In such a climate alone, a worker can develop his potential to the maximum.

The motivation and capacity for productivity is not something that management or anybody else can give to the worker. He has it within himself. But, neither the obvious forces of authority nor the subtle forces of diplomacy will bring it out. It can emerge only in a climate of freedom — freedom to express one's ability to the full, to participate in a common task, to be recognised for what one is and does and to grow and develop in terms of one's basic potentials. This is exactly what motivates management itself. When it recognises the play of these urges in the worker, it will create a pattern of relationship that will truly be conducive to productivity.

In conclusion, basic, three facts must be remembered:

(1) More important than what management gives is what workers want.

(2) More important than what management gives is what workers see as receiving.

(3) More important than what management gives is the way in which it is given.

# Assessment of Men

# 13

## INTRODUCTION

In industry men have to be assessed for a variety of reasons but chiefly for selection, promotion, and transfer. The goal is to control men through knowledge about them.

Selection is one aspect of the total process of recruitment. Recruitment aims at attracting competent men to perform specific tasks in industry. It calls for a knowledge of job requirements, sources of labour, channels and agencies through which labour can be obtained, various steps in the selection procedure, etc. The chart indicates these steps. As can be seen, the structured interview is one of them.

Preliminary Interview
Investigation of Previous History
Employment Tests
Structured Interview
Approval by Department Head
Medical Examination
Placement

The structured interview is most useful when used along with other selection techniques. It is the most important single step on the selection ladder. It can also be used to gather information from an outgoing or retiring employee, for the purpose of follow-up of various personnel and training programmes and generally before making any administrative decision. The structured interview is also called the 'patterned', 'directive' or 'controlled' interview, it consists of a standardized form on which various categories for judging an applicant are stated. These are structured to cover both background as well as current information about the interviewee. Categories include family background, educational background, work experience, health, personal appearance, manners, expression, tact and sensitivity, drive and initiative, etc. The type of questions related to these categories may be suggested by the application and the personal data form of the applicant.

The structured interview provides information in a systematic manner. Because the categories on which information is sought are laid down, such an interview also promotes uniform performance from various interviewers in case a board interview is involved. On the other hand, because it is structured it does not encourage free inhibited responses from interviewees. The approach is somewhat mechanical and the battery of uniform questions for all interviewees fails to take into account the unique character of each of them.

## COMMON PITFALLS AND BIASES

*Personal bias of the interviewer.* This refers to the tendency of the interviewer to make a decision about the applicant on the basis of some personal mannerism or characteristic. Interviewers often make adverse decisions about those interviewed on the basis of traits not related to job success. As for instance, 'talking with cigarette in hand', 'loudclothing, foreign looking' etc.

*Bias may also be contagious.* This happens particularly in board interviews where the reactions of the chairman or any dominant member of the board are taken over by other interviewers.

*Bias may also be related to physical stereotypes.* Scientific studies show little relationship between big forehead and intelligence, inability to look one in the eye and honesty, protruding lips and cruelty, etc. The wording of questions may also introduce bias either by using words which are not well understood by interviewees or by using questions with suggestive answers.

## SUGGESTIONS FOR IMPROVING EFFECTIVENESS OF STRUCTURED INTERVIEWS

1. Establish rapport or good relationship with interviewees.

2. Keep in mind specifications of the job in order not to be off the course or be side-tracked by the interviewee's personality, habits or interests.

3. Know what can and cannot be determined from the interviewee.

4. Pay attention to the physical comforts of the interviewee. Give and keep appointments. See that he is not kept waiting. Maintain privacy of the interview. Do not appear to be busy with something else whilst conducting the interview.

5. Allow for the hesitancy of the interviewee's responses. Do not make notes whilst interviewee is speaking but record impressions immediately after he leaves.

6. Opening the interview is a skill in itself. The interviewer must have the ability to put people at ease. Brief informal chat on any topic of mutual interest or a humorous remark may put the interviewee at ease.

7. Interpreting responses of interviewees is a difficult task. Interpretation may be through direct observation of appearance, (grooming, poise, self-expression etc.) or may be through inference drawn from what the interviewee states. In either case the interviewer must be careful not to project himself into the situation.

8. After the interview is over, watch for free post interview reactions. Often the interviewee feels relaxed after the interview is over and may make reactions that are vital in assessing him.

## MERIT RATING METHOD

Merit rating, sometimes, called employee evaluation, employee rating, efficiency rating, progress report, personnel review etc., is a systematic periodic evaluation of the worth of an individual to an establishment, usually made by someone in position to observe his performance.

Evaluation is obligatory. The question is not whether or not to evaluate but whether evaluation is to be haphazard, random and irresponsible or systematic and objective.

### Purpose

1. Promotion and Transfer — Chief difficulty comes from unions, even those which are otherwise co-operative.

2. Employee Improvement — Analysis of strong and weak points to develop an employee through training and counselling.

3. Personnel Research — Evaluating personnel practices.

### Advantages

1. Helps build up morale through confidence in the fairness of management.

2. Reveals weaknesses that facilitate on-the-job-training and brings hidden abilities into the open.

3. Whatever recommendations a rater makes, if substantiated by a factual record are more likely to be taken in the right spirit. Transfers become more acceptable.

4. Merit Rating provides supervisors with both basis for and the necessary training in developing counselling skill.

5. The fairness, severity or leniency with which supervisors evaluate their men can be judged by management.

6. Dealings with union can be placed on more objective basis.

### Limitations

The use of rating scale does not do away with subjective judgements. The scale only helps to make these judgements as accurate and reliable as possible. Pitfalls can be minimized through guides — technical, dynamic, and interpretive.

## MERIT RATING FORMS AND GUIDES

### 1. Selection of items

Traits selected for inclusion in the rating form should be characteristic of the work actually performed. Usually one type of rating form is used for the supervisory staff and another for workers and/or non-supervisory and non-technical staff. The traits selected should not overlap. An omnibus form is also sometimes used.

One way of determining traits or items in a scale would be either to carry out job analysis or determine the critical requirements of the job.

Inclusion of many traits does not necessarily make the scale a good one.

Merit Rating Forms usually include the following:

1. Job knowledge
2. Accuracy, efficiency and regularity of work performance
3. Relational skills
4. Work attitude or personal traits

Often information about the standards of performance expected of employees is obtained from the supervisors.

### 2. Instructions on Filling in the Rating Scale

Besides mechanical information on how to fill in the form, raters must be informed on the following:

Raters may be trained to recall specific instances in support of generalizations. Raters have to be trained on the necessity of being free from the authoritarian influence of others or of their own past. Raters have to guard against the 'generosity error'. If raters have definite objections towards filling in the scale these should be discussed before rating.

Raters must realize that the various grading of traits are not absolute values. Grading should be against the background of normal expectancy level.

Raters must be aware of the extent of work opportunity given to demonstrate ratees' potential for a given trait.

Raters must remember that the standard of rating will vary from one rating period to another.

Raters must realize that rating scales are confidential documents and not to be discussed or treated lightly.

Raters must be clear about the operational meaning of abstract terms (viz., loyalty, leadership, etc.) used in describing ratees.

### 3. Interpreting Merit Ratings Forms

Merit Ratings have many purposes. Be clear as to which one of them you have in mind.

The usual practice is not to tie ratings directly to administrative decisions.

The profile revealed by a rating scale does not permit passing a final judgment about the ratees. A rating scale is one of the aids in making reliable decisions.

Be cautious in comparing ratings of men in different departments. The average for these various groups may vary from one department to another.

Evaluation of merit rating profiles will change, as information is gathered about the reliability (consistency) and validity (accuracy) of the scale over a period of time.

In discussing results with ratees' start by stressing good points, follow with what's wrong in the record and conclude with other good points. Locating mistakes is not enough. The employee must be helped through discussion, special training, etc., to correct his weakness.

Although pooled ratings of more than one rater usually increase the reliability of the results, this cannot be automatically assumed in all cases.

Studies of research made elsewhere do not permit us to assume similar relationships in one's own plant.

## PLANNING AND EXECUTING A MERIT RATING PROGRAMME

### Introduction

Merit Rating calls for comprehensive planning.

Be clear about the purpose of Merit Rating — administrative, research or diagnostic.

Be aware of the necessity to inform ratees on how they are being rated. Therapeutic follow-up work calls for the passing of this information.

An important question is: Who should rate — superiors, peers or subordinates? The latter two types of ratings are uncommon but researches indicate that in a good group they have not been less accurate. Since (a) peers come into closer contact with each other, (b) they see not only a ratees's best side only, (c) one gets a number of judgements the average of which is likely to be more reliable, peer rating is often found helpful.

Another important question is: How often to rate monthly, quarterly or annually? Six months is considered a good interval. If ratings are taken too often, the time taken creates resistance or indifference. Special ratings may be made at critical times. Ratings may also be done when services are terminated or a transfer effected.

The time factor: Top management should spare time for Merit Rating give time to raters for a systematic rating and stagger the distribution of the Merit Rating Forms.

Who will plan and execute the programme? The planning is usually done by the personnel department and the execution is often entrusted to a qualified personnel technician.

Often, before the Merit Rating Form is constructed and the programme launched, some information about the standards of performance expected of employees is obtained from the supervisors. These standards are discussed with subordinates and then structured by the personnel department for constructing the form.

The form itself may combine more than one type of Merit Rating techniques. Often management prefers not to summarize the Rating Form into a single index to avoid competitive comparisons. A profile is used for diagnostic purpose.

An open-end Evaluation Report from the supervisor is sometimes called forth to supplement and sometimes check upon information obtained through the Form.

Sometimes, personnel men interview the supervisor using the patterned interview technique for checking up latter's ratings.

### Pilot try-out

Both to test the plan and to train the raters, an initial try-out is recommended and may be combined with an initial attempt to determine the worthwhileness of the Form.

Some of the topics to be studied in the try-out period are: (1) Reliability (2) Validity (3) Distribution — Is there an adequate spread? (4) Halo Effect — Tendency of one or two traits to influence the ratings given to other traits (5) Variation in ratings of individual raters and between various departments (6) Relationship of ratings to age of ratees, length of time they have been in the present job, etc.

Results of the try-out may be discussed with the experimental group as well as with larger group of supervisors and their opinions called forth.

### Selling the programme

Letters, notices, manuals, individual conferences, group conferences, etc., are some of the methods of selling the programme.

### Training to raters

Individual and group instructions, printed guides, practice ratings, etc., are some of the methods. Lack of an adequate training programme is the principal source of weakness in a Rating Programme. The deficiency usually lies not so much in the tool as in the user of the tool.

Training should have two goals:

(1) Raters must be made to realize the value and importance of Rating Scales.

(2) Raters must be taught both, how to rate and interpret the Rating Form after it is filled.

Training can be made effective by:

(1) Having top management to endorse and propagate the Merit Rating Programme.

(2) Through discussions etc., with raters to give a feeling of participation in the Merit Rating Scheme.

(3) Delegation of raters may be sent to other companies to investigate and report back.

(4) By making training a continuous process.

In determining the content of the training programme find out first what the raters have to do, both in terms of technical details about filling in the form, the dynamics of filling it in and the technique of interpretation and use of Rating Scales.

## Using Merit Rating Results

*Progress Interview:* This interview is held by the supervisor for his ratee to help the latter check upon and improve his performance. In conducting such an interview:

(a) Be clear as to what you expect of the man as an employee.

(b) Decide on the time and place. Carefully review the form.

(c) Put the employee at ease. Be friendly.

(d) Talk about his good qualities first. Then cover each point in detail including his weaknesses. Conclude with other good points in his record.

(e) Do not compare ratee with others but you may compare his own past and present performance and what you expect of him.

(f) Discuss practical ways and means of removing his weaknesses or improving his performance. Where information is needed and readily available give this to the ratee. If not so readily available arrange for getting it.

(g) Encourage ratee to express his reaction. Any opportunity for expression is always welcome.

(h) Avoid giving direct advice. Except in extreme cases, the ratee does not have to improve unless he himself so desires.

(i) Limit the interview to about an hour or so.

(j) After the interview is over, fill in the form for record of interviewer. This may either be discussed with departmental head or head of personnel. A copy of records must go to the personnel department for reference and research.

## Evaluating the Merit Rating Form

Evaluation usually moves over a period of time.

A. Methods of determining validity (How well does the Scale measure, what it is supposed to measure):

(i) Comparison with some direct, measurement of performance, e.g., production record. Most definite but least practical since one cannot measure relational skill and like traits, directly.

(ii) Comparison with psychological tests purporting to measure the same ability.

(iii) Comparison with work samples. Not suitable at supervisory level.

(iv) Analysis of the distribution of rating scale. Results should conform to the shape of the normal curve.

(v) Follow-up procedure: After ratings are obtained they may be compared with the progress of the individual in the organization over a period of time, say a year or two. Good as a research method but not useful when the ratings are used to influence the future of the individual. This procedure has been, however, widely used.

B. Methods of determining reliability (How consistently does the scale measure whatever it is measuring):

(i) Comparisons of re-ratings.

(ii) Agreement existing between the ratings of independent raters. Whether this is a measure of reliability (consistency of response) or validity, such an agreement increases the value of the scale and is desirable.

## MANAGERIAL PERFORMANCE APPRAISAL

Since the introduction of scientific management in industry, attempts have been made by various social scientists and organization men to develop and implement an objective performance appraisal system for managerial staff. Doubts, however, have consistently been raised about efficacy of these performance appraisals. As the appraisals have been done by the human beings, the elimination of elements of subjectivity has almost been impossible. However, efforts have been made to minimise the subjectivity aspect. A practical model thus, is being suggested here though the possibilities of certain aspects of subjectivity may not be totally eliminated yet this model may bring about fair amount of objectivity in the system. The recommended model is described as follows:

1. Organizations have definite goal — long-term and short-term. The goals are split into sub-goals and specific group of people with a leader is assigned the job of fulfilment of the sub-goal. The final responsibility for fulfilment of their goal lies on the entire team but the leader in the process has to play a crucial role. It is a fashion of the day for social scientists to plead that, performance appraisals should only be meant for developmental needs and not for using it for the purpose of reward. To me, it seems to be highly theoretical and impracticable. After all, development and growth itself is a reward given to a person in an organization. The performance appraisal, therefore, most adequately reflects and identifies both the potential of the person, his developmental needs and also based on his past performance, the reward package both extrinsic and intrinsic. The model which is being described perhaps meets both these requirements.

1. At the beginning of each year, the target in the given situation with all possible inputs and other infrastructure should be set jointly by the subordinates (the ratee), his boss (the rater) and the divisional head (the reviewer). These three persons must examine in detail the expectations from the ratee as also resources that are required and placed at his disposal.
2. The performance of the ratee should be reviewed in light of inputs given consistently between reviewer, rater and ratee. The records must be maintained of the proceedings of these meetings.

3. The review of the performance should be done in every 2-3 months jointly and again records of the proceedings be maintained.
4. In a year atleast 4 reviews must take place and records maintained.
5. The ratee must be free to bringforth the problems that he faces in an effort to fulfil or exceeed the target.
6. At the end of the year, on the basis of performance as recorded throughout the year, appraisal of the ratee should be done in his presence.
7. In the event of any disagreement amongst the ratee, rater and reviewer, documents, etc. should be referred to top management for giving final appraisal to the ratee.
8. It would be worthwhile if top management directly holds dialogue with the ratee in presence of rater if the performance is adversely commented upon. The performance appraisal thus, made should not remain on the records for its glorification. It must be examined by the HRD and again plans initiated for training and development of the ratee.
9. Both, ratee and reviewer should be given intensive training with regard to the techniques of the evaluation and appraisal. This will eliminate avoidable subjectivity.
10. It will also be worthwhile to get the assessment of rater and reviewer of the ratees. This cross-assessment may create awareness about their strengths and weakness to enable the organization plans for their development.
11. The departmental and divisional heads in key positions should be appraised by their peers who have the functional relationship. This cross-checking of perceptions of each other is cumbersome, no doubt, but surely in practice it will eliminate the much maligned trait of human beings, i.e., subjectivity.
12. Performance appraisal form should be made as simple and understandable as possible. Vague criteria create confusion and they are interpreted differently by different persons at different levels. This can be avoided.

13. Performance appraisal is always done in a hurry and that too under pressure from the top management. This vital work receives least priority. The sincere and deliberate thought is given to see through the rater's strength first. Tendency is always to pinpoint the weaknesses. The present model will eliminate this problem.
14. Raters and reviewers must realise that their primary duty is to help subordinates to develop. An effort thus directed, should receive one of the top priorities in boss's checklist. The leader must show leadership so that subordinates can respond to the challenges of the organizations, voluntarily and wilfully.

# Behaviour of the Leader

# 14

One of the most often asked questions in the arena of leadership behaviour is, how should a leader conduct himself in order to maintain the moving equilibrium in his group? In an attempt to answer this, a few rules or maxims for leader's behaviour could be enumerated. As it would be enormous to include all the rules or maxims that operate, it would, perhaps, be sufficient to mention only those which are concerned with the position of the leader and the nature of his authority. While the maxims mentioned herein may sound rather familiar being experienced from generation to generation centring around leadership of one kind or the other, the conclusions drawn up would be quite close to the contemporary realities.

In view of extremely complicated nature of human behaviour and thought patterns, while it may not be possible to speak the final word on the maxims of leadership, the attempt would be to provide general guidelines to the analysis of leadership behaviour to examine or predict the effectiveness or otherwise of the leader in a given situation. Precisely, such maxims, therefore, provide a checklist instead of the guiding rules.

In this context, it would be unrealistic to assume that the leader who has followed religiously these maxims shall be leading himself to success. Instead, towards achieving the goal set for himself and the members of the group he is leading, the leader must respond positively and intelligently to the demands of the situation he is in for the time being. His personal discretion — instead of referring to these maxims — must always obtain priority to enable him to take up the situation he is facing with at any given time.

## Rules of Leadership

The leader maintains his own position. A leader cannot successfully lead his group unless he is established as a person from whom authority and orders flow. The leader will be obeyed without being questioned by members of his group, if the leader is a person in the structure of authority.

If, therefore, a leader is to originate interaction for a group, he must establish and maintain his rank. Leader, especially, if he is new to a group, should wait until he has established his own position before he tries to reach his objectives. This may mean delay, but here as in so many other aspects of leadership, delay in the beginning means speed in the end.

### Leader and the group norms

The leader must live up to the norms of his group. Every group has its norms according to which the members of the group behave. Acceptability of a person by a group depends on the person's behaviour which should be according to the accepted norms of the group.

It has also been seen that the person of the highest social rank in a group is the person who comes close to realising in his behaviour the norms of the group and even the lowest of the group finds enough of it in the leader. Any failure on the part of the leader to live up to the group norms undermines his own social rank. The leader must also be as zealous as anyone else in obeying his own order. The old command, "Do as I say, not as I do" is fatal to leadership. The leader, in fact, must set an example.

### Initiative

The leader must lead. The leader should not only live up to the norms of his group, but he should be able to lead his group even to change the norms.

Being the person who originates interaction for other members of the group, any failure on the part of the leader to originate interaction or to take the initiative will make him that much less a leader. Whenever a choice to make the next move lies before a group, the members expect him to take action. The leader after consultation with the members should take the initiative to guide and lead them regarding future course of action. People, in fact, do not object to clear, firm and specific orders. Rather they welcome orders in any situation in which they deem orders appropriate.

### Quality of order

The leader must not give orders that will not be obeyed. This rule is the converse of the last. If a leader must give orders when they are expected and will be obeyed, he must not give orders when they will not and cannot be obeyed. The distinction of these situations is, wherein the sensitivity of the leader lies.

When the leader gives orders that are not obeyed, he has by the fact undermined his rank. His social rank is in mutual dependence with the authority of his orders. Orders of leader disobeyed will make the members presumptuous regarding obeying his future orders. It would, hence, lead the members of the group in doubt regarding the competence of the leader.

### Use of established channels

Another important aspect is the role played by the leader in maintaining the position of others in the group. It is found that though the leader interacts with every member of the group, he interacts most often with the persons nearest to him in social ranks. The orders of the leader tend to be transmitted to the group through these men, the so-called 'lieutenants'. The leader by not transmitting his orders through his lieutenants, throws doubt on the presumption that the lieutenant's orders are to be obeyed, as one of the factors determining a lieutenant's social rank is his interaction with the leader.

The leader should maintain the social rank of his lieutenants so that their orders are obeyed which, in fact, are his own orders, transmitted through them. Undermining lieutenant's authority, in fact, culminates in undermining his own authority in turn. It is, hence, in favour of the leader himself, not "to jump the line".

### Social felicitations

The leader must not thrust himself upon his followers on social occasions.

To say that the leader must not thrust himself upon his followers does not mean that he should not interact with them at all. He should make efforts to "know his men". On occasion of social gatherings the leader should make it a point to attend them, but should avoid behaving like a person in authority. More than any other member of the group, the leader must be flexible in his pattern of interaction.

### Projection of group members

The leader must neither blame nor, always, praise a particular member of his group before other members. The leader has much to do with establishing the social rank of his followers. When he blames a man in public, he is lowering or attempting to lower the man's social rank, that is the degree of esteem in which he is held by the members of the group. But, the leader is not the only man who determines social rank; the opinions of the other members count, too. They may not be ready to accept the leader's evaluation. When he blames a follower in public, he is not only humiliating the man; he may also be putting his own reputation for justice and his capacity for living up to the norms of the group in doubt. Moreover if, the person he blames is one of his lieutenants, he is impugning the source through which his own orders will pass, and therefore helping to destroy the line of authority. It is not generally recognised that the same argument that applies to blame applies also to praise. Occasional public praise of a man is admirable, but frequent praise may embarrass him, because it may show that the leader is giving him an evaluation that the rest of the group is not ready to accept. Praise is an important factor for motivation, but it should be done discretely.

### Comprehensive perspective

The leader must take into consideration the total situation. A leader's conduct for maintenance of moving equilibrium in his group should vary from situation to situation, as no one situation is similar to another. Leader's success will depend upon his perception of the total situation and diagnosis of the problem arising out of it. Hence, it is the 'total situation' which should be taken into consideration by the leader.

The total situation would include the following:

(1) The environment, both physical and social. The latter including the larger groups of which the group itself is a part and the groups of which it is not a part, but with which it is in contact;

(2) The materials, tools and techniques with which the group operates on the environment;

(3) The external systems, that is, the relations between the members of the group necessary for group action on the environment;

(4) The internal system that is the social equations that elaborate upon the external system and react upon it; and

(5) The norms of the group — in the effort to maintain a moving equilibrium the leader should remember that as the factors are mutually dependent, a change in any one of these factors will, in general, bring about changes in the others, for which he may have to allow and compensate.

### Regulatory functions

In maintaining discipline the leader must be less concerned with inflicting punishment than with creating the conditions in which the group will discipline itself. The more the punishment is inflicted by the leader, the more the leader has to inflict. Leaders, at times, are led astray by the fallacy that a man disobeys orders out of sheer perversity. Usually, there are more compelling reasons why the orders are disobeyed, though the man may not be aware of them, if the man is punished without considering or changing the reasons, the reasons will persist and lead the man to disobey the leader again, while his resentment of the punishment the leader has inflicted will give him still further reasons for disobedience. He will want to get back at the leader and he now knows how he can make him angry.

When something has gone wrong in the group, the leader should better take aside the man who is apparently responsible and instead of bowling him out, ask him to explain how the mistake was made and how it can be avoided another time. The leader will then accomplish several useful results, (a) He will escape the danger of punishing an innocent person, (b) If the man who seems to be responsible is in fact responsible, the leader will avoid humiliating him and hurting his standing in the group, (c) The leader may begin to learn what the underlying difficulty is, (d) By asking the man to explain what happened, the leader may be taking the most effective step towards preventing the mistake from happening again. In the course of his explanation the man may begin to see the underlying difficulty for himself. As seeing is the first step towards correcting, he may try to correct himself in future.

### Ability to listen

A leader should be well informed in a situation about the situation, if he has to lead successfully. For gathering of information he should be a careful and receptive listener.

Although the leader is placed at the centre of a web of communication in his group and, therefore, is in a good position to get information, he will not get it just because the communication channels exist. The real question is how they are to be used. Everybody talks about the importance of two-way communication in an organization — the importance of communication from follower to leader as well as from leader to follower, but few people know as to what shall be communicated and how communication upward shall be encouraged. In the relationship between leader and follower, it is found that two opposing forces are at work. On one hand, a follower naturally seeks interaction with a leader he admires; on the other hand, authority tends to cut down interaction between the leader and the follower and make the follower's attitude distant and respectful rather than close and friendly. Between equals in an organisation an easy give-and-take will tend to build itself up without deliberated contrivance. There is little to prevent it. But the leader cannot assume that free communication from his followers to him will come naturally.

A leader cannot solve the problem merely by saying that he is always ready to see his followers and that "his door is always open". He must seek interaction with his followers. This may seem to conflict with the rule that the leader should not thrust himself upon his followers on social occasions. Whereas it is not as it applies to situations in which several of the followers have gathered and it will not be violation if he seeks interaction with each of his followers alone. When the leader seeks an opportunity for interaction, his purpose should be to pass the time of day with the follower and show that he, the leader, is friendly and interested. In short, the leader must, if he is to receive communication, show by his actions that the channels are open.

Being a good listener will help the leader in following ways, firstly, he will be better informed about various aspects of the whole situation, viz., technical and social, facing his group. The leader should remember that the problems which are important for his followers are equally important to him. Secondly, the follower's thinking will change while he talks. As he talks about his own problems and those of his group, he will see the problems more clearly which would mark the first step towards his effective action. The leader will have to give fewer orders himself if the other members of the group have seen for themselves what the orders ought to be. Control will be decentralised. Thirdly, that nothing increases the respect and gratitude of one man for another, more than the other's listening to him fully and with interest. This is part of the phenomenon the Freudians call transference. And finally, the encouragement of free communication on one occasion will lead to still freer communication on another as communication feeds on communication.

### Self cognition

The leader must know himself. Leaders of groups know most of these rules which have been stated either by intimation or by conscious awareness. And yet, they are often violated. As Ovid said long ago, "We see the better path and we approve of it, but we take the worse". From all that has gone before, it should be obvious that the leader himself is the greatest threat to the moving equilibrium of the group. He can do most to put it in jeopardy. He may be the most active member of the group and yet, he must often keep silent. He must live up to the norms of the group and yet he, more than anyone else, should resolve conflicts of norms. More than anyone else he has the ends of the group at heart. He must be under great self-control in a situation where control is difficult. If, therefore, he must know his men well, he must know himself still better. He must know the passions in him that, unchecked, will destroy him as a leader, and he must know their sources in his personality. For how can one control a force, the source of whose energy one does not know? Self-knowledge is the first step in self-control.

# Changing Attitudes

# 15

Attitude has been defined as "readiness to act in a certain way". It is a set or 'frame of reference' towards or against people and situations. This 'set' may also be directed towards one's own self. As a matter of fact the way an individual looks at himself forms the most important 'frame of reference' that guides his reactions. This selective reaction tendency to the 'me' and the 'mine' determines the way an individual looks at life including the work situation. This is a focus of attention that management often misses.

Whether an employee approaches the work situation with positive or negative attitude, depends upon whether or not there is self-involvement and whether such involvement enhances or threatens the self. Managers would do well to remember that a man's most absorbing interest is himself. If this interest can be used to make the employee look at himself as he is, rather than as he believes he is, many unrealistic attitudes and seemingly difficult problems in the relational field can be resolved. The discrepancy between what an employee experiences and what he believes he is experiencing is the most important factor that leads to confusion, prejudices, resistance and consequent maladjustment. A skilful manager can create a social climate of acceptance and permissiveness in which an employee would feel free to look at himself as he is, therefore, feel free to acknowledge his mistakes and be open to new ideas and attitudes.

For many reasons managers otherwise competent, find it difficult to create a social climate in which employees feel free to look at themselves. When an employee brings a problem or raises an objection, the most common reaction is either to ignore him, belittle his problems, patronise him or advise him. Experiences both in psychological laboratories and on the factory floor have shown these approaches to be ineffective.

Below are listed certain general findings and specific techniques in handling employees' problems. Implied in these principles and techniques are certain attitudes. Researches indicate that if these attitudes are not actually experienced (understood and accepted) by the manager, using these techniques, their mechanical applications do not bring about the desired results.

### General Findings

Attitudinal learning is self-motivated. It is never given; always caught.

Attitudinal learning is more an emotional activity than an intellectual one. Hence, it depends more on what one experiences as a total person than what one verbally accepts.

Attitudinal learning is more 'do-learning' than 'new learning'. It is chiefly freedom from yesterdays' conditionings.

It is difficult to locate any conscious discernible process involved in change of attitudes. The change is of the nature of insight — a sudden new perception of people and situation.

There is no solution to personal problems in the sense that two plus two make four. Personal problems such as frustration are not being promoted, envy of another's superior skill, sense of insecurity about one's future, fear of loss of status etc. are problems that can be resolved not by seeking a verbal solution but by changing one's perception of these problems. In other words by a change in one's own attitude towards the problem.

Attitudinal changes are difficult because certain fears and anxieties appear to have no real grounds.

This is so because many deep-rooted fears exist within the individual, outside the threshold of his conscious mind. Unresolved frustrations, accumulated resentments that have remained unexpressed, humiliations and failures over the years, all exert their cumulative pressure upon the individual. The individual himself may be vaguely aware or even totally unaware of these forces, yet their power to disturb remains undiminished and makes his emotional balance precarious.

In these circumstances even trivial events (a slight change in work procedure, change in designation, appointment of a new boss) arouse a disproportionately powerful reaction. The way to deal with the problem is to raise the total self awareness of the individual by accepting him as he is. If this awareness increases and he begins to accept more and more of himself, his capacity to deal objectively with problems also increases.

### Specific techniques

I. *Face to face with an employee's problem — Be a good listener.* Listening is one of the most difficult skill to learn. It does not merely involve keeping silent when the other speaks. One's attitude must reflect sincere interest in what is said. When the other man speaks many of us are busy manufacturing counter-arguments in our mind. This belies listening.

One must listen not only to what is expressed but also to what is left unexpressed. In other words, learn to listen between the words.

If enough time is not available, do not give appointment to the employee. One cannot listen with an eye on the watch.

The fact of listening must be communicated to the employee. Make him feel that for the time being he is the only person you are interested in.

After he starts speaking do not interrupt him. Do not try to meet part of his problems or grievances. Let him tell the whole story. Once you relax and let him blow off the steam, both are ready to get to work.

II. *Experience unconditional positive regard and acceptance of the employee.* Listening establishes genuine relationship. As the employee starts talking, the problem begins to emerge, it is the function of the executive counsellor to help the employee recognise and accept these feelings as they arise. The greater the extent of self-revelation the more the chances for spontaneous insight to emerge.

Self-revelation, however, is painful. It is safer not to recognise feelings of hostility and jealousy of fear and inadequacy within one-self. It has been repeatedly observed, however, that if the executive-counsellor feels and expresses non-judgemental acceptance of the employee ("*Whatever you are it is O.K. with me*") then the employee takes over the same approach towards his own feelings and attitudes.

Non-judgemental acceptance can be expressed through the following techniques:

(1) **The technique of 'minimal structuring'**. Put a guiding question and encourage the employee to talk. Do not

structure the interview either by guiding, judging, advising, or interpreting what he says.

(2) **The technique of 'reflection of feelings'**. Reflection means handing back. Select the most significant feelings expressed and either re-state them or show by words or gesture that you recognise and accept the fact of these feelings, but have no judgment to pass. This can be done simply by saying hmm or even by nodding.

(3) **The technique of picking up important responses and calling for elaboration.** This very often has the effect of saying: "take back these responses of yours and kindly re-examine them".

When an employee discovers that he is in a social climate where he can reveal himself, as he is, the need for defences disappears. If this can happen, the face saving devices, the mechanism of justification, the mood of righteousness etc. begin to crumble. The employee is enabled to look at the problem objectively. This openness is absolutely essential before a problem can be tackled. But once the emphasis shifts from self-justification and self-defence to the problem itself, a scientific approach becomes possible. Non-judgemental acceptance brings about this shift.

III. Assuming that hindering attitudes are minimised, an objective approach to the problem is now possible. The various steps outlined below do not necessarily follow in a consecutive sequence.

The most important step in the direction of handling problems is to gather all the facts as the employee sees them and then weigh the evidence he presents. If there is merit in what he states, be prepared to recognise it.

Determine what the employee wants to gain. Reach an agreement to his exact purpose or intention.

Tell truthfully your side of the picture. Show how your company's policies, technical requirements and the time factor stand in relation to the resolution of the problem.

Compare your side of the picture with that of the employee. If possible, encourage him to make the comparisons, pointing out where necessary, the way in which his interest will be effected.

Do not be afraid to say "no" provided you give reasons for saying so. If you have been able to develop good relationship and confidence in your men there are chances that a negative reply will be taken in a proper spirit.

Do not 'pass the buck', nothing is more irritating to the employee than the executive who will not decide. If you do not have the authority to settle a grievance, you should not handle it. However, avoid snap judgements, it indicates a closed mind.

As you meet the employee's problems, be aware of your own psychological reactions. If you have made a mistake, recognise it and be willing to admit it. If you do it gracefully, it will make clear to the employee the fact of your personal integrity and help in establishing a better relationship.

# Conference Leadership

16

When a group of people meet together to pool knowledge, opinions and experiences in order to solve a problem, we have a conference.

A conference is not just a meeting. A shareholders' meeting or a meeting addressed by a lecturer does not constitute a conference. A conference involves a process of constructive participation on the part of individual members guided by a leader.

The conference leader directs and controls the group so as to enable it to accomplish its purpose. A good (democratic) leader neither dominates the group nor permits it to be so disorganized as to fail to define and reach its goal.

The conference in industry is an important channel of communication. Specifically, it serves as a tool of training, as a means of changing attitudes, for the purpose of exchanging information and encouraging creative ideas and as an instrument for solving problems and resolving conflicts.

The following general rules will help a conference member to get the most out of a conference:

(1) Give prior thought to the topic to be discussed.

(2) Do not come to the conference with a blank mind.

(3) Listen. Try to understand another's viewpoints. Do not accept or reject immediately. Instead, give considered attention to what is said, not only by the leader but by every other member in the conference.

(4) Express your ideas. Do not hold them back. If you do not understand what is discussed or disagree with what is said, do not hesitate to call for clarification either from the leader or other members. However, avoid monopolising the discussion.

(5) Be brief and stick to the point.

## LEADING A CONFERENCE

### Pre-Conference Preparation

A competent conference leader tries to acquire as thorough a knowledge as he can about the subject matter to be discussed.

He next prepares the discussion plan. Such a plan must include the specific goal of the conference, the manner in which the topic is to be introduced, the sequences in which the subject matter can best be discussed, key problems that members will have to solve, questions and illustrations that might stimulate members to think, possible implications of decisions arrived at, etc.

Preparation must also include some knowledge about individual members. A group that is homogeneous in training, background and experience is more effective than one that is heterogeneous. Each participant must be notified well in advance and whenever required be given necessary materials to enable him to prepare for the conference.

The physical requirements for conducting the conference should not be ignored. Proper seating arrangements, ventilation, charts, films, case study materials, paper and pencil, name-tags etc., are factors that a good leader must not lose sight of.

### Approach

Approach refers to the way in which the leader opens the conference.

Do not offer the opening remarks unless you have got the attention of the group. Start off with something that would capture the interest of the group, viz., a story, a humorous anecdote, a case history, a thought provoking or dramatic statement, etc.

Define the topic and outline the scope of discussion. It is often a good practice to write definitions on the board.

Indicate briefly the procedure to be followed.

At these points the conference actually starts.

### Getting Maximum Participation

There can be no conference without participation. For the leader, one way to bring out adequate responses is to recede into the background.

The use of questions is another excellent way to draw out members. Questions may be 'direct' (addressed to single member) or 'overhead' (addressed to the group as a whole). Questions may be asked to open the discussion, to gather facts, to provoke thinking, to develop the subject to the next stage, to change the trend of discussion, to call attention to a point that has been left out, to prevent the group from digressing, to take attention away from personal remarks, etc. In asking questions, the leader must remember the following points:

(1) Encourage complete answers. Allow for the hesitancy of the members in replying to questions.

(2) Do not let every body answer at the same time.

(3) Do not allow a few to take over the monopoly of answering. Tactfully bring in others. You may use direct questions for this purpose.

(4) When an answer is an expression of mere like or dislike and reflects the prejudice of a member, ask for further elaboration.

(5) Ask for questions that can be answered. They must stimulate thinking but must not be so difficult as to discourage it.

(6) Questions must be put in a way that is clear and simple.

Maximum participation is also facilitated by promoting friendly and informal relationship between members of the group. The leader can help by not making himself the centre of the group.

The way in which the leader treats members, the extent of self-control displayed by him, his sincerity, impartiality and friendliness would go a long way in promoting good relationship between group members.

### Conducting the Actual Discussion

The conference often starts by the leader presenting facts or problems.

If participation is adequate, many difficult and even contradictory responses will emerge. A democratic leader not only accepts the right of individual members to put forth their ideas but communicates this acceptance in certain ways like nodding his head, attentively listening to what is said thereby indirectly encouraging others to listen to the speaker, etc.

Acceptance, however, does not imply license. While accepting the right of expression, the leader regulates responses of members so as to move the discussion towards the group goal. One way to do this is to restructure the responses. A group member may put forth ideas in a hesitant longwinding and disorganized manner. After encouraging him to come out with the responses, the leader must have the ability to re-state the responses briefly and clearly. A useful technique is to put the restructured idea on the blackboard. This will help him to organize and combine responses as they emerge from the group.

Members are apt to either state irrelevant points or repeat the same thought in different words. When these are re-stated by the leader, irrelevant ideas and repetitions become obvious and they can then be set aside. Basic ideas may then be regrouped and written on the blackboard for evaluation by the group.

In evaluating responses, the leader must encourage members not to pass judgements or take sides but, to consider the alternatives objectively. This is a difficult thing to do and can be best done indirectly. As for example the leader may himself refrain from either justifying or condemning a proposition. This does not, however, prevent him from evaluating the responses by mustering all the arguments for and against the proposition. The difference between evaluation and judgement is that the latter carries overtones of condemnations or defences whereas the former is free from both and is concerned with collecting facts. If the conference moves smoothly, recommendations or solutions will emerge spontaneously. The leader must carefully summarise these and if necessary, find out a line of action. It may be necessary to summarise ideas at various stages of the discussion and finally arrive at a final summary. Whatever conclusions are arrived at, they must be satisfying to the group as a whole and must not be superimposed by the leader.

A record of work done at each conference including manner in which the conference took place and final conclusions arrived at, must be maintained.

## HANDLING DIFFICULT MEMBERS

A variety of techniques for controlling various types of difficult members is outlined below. The competent leader will choose one or more of these to meet the situation.

### 1. The chronic objector

Try and locate the reasons for his hostility and if possible remove them.

Try and re-word his objections so as to get to the theme that disturbs him.

If he continues to irritate others, throw his objections to the group members and let them manage him.

Deliberately pass over what he says.

### 2. Continuous talker

Tactfully interrupt him and ask others to comment on what he says.

If he responds so quickly that others get no opportunity to participate, turn your questions deliberately to others and fail to recognise him. As a last resort request him to give others a chance.

### 3. Shy or timid member

Make him participate addressing him deliberately by his name. Ask a question that he can easily answer and compliment him when he makes a good point.

### 4. Disinterested member

Ask direct questions related to his work. If possible touch open topics in which he is interested and ask for his advice. If you know something of what he has said or done that is helpful, hold it up as an example to other members without appearing to flatter him.

### 5. Member who uses abusive language, makes personal remarks about others or shows lack of good manners

If you know about such a member being in the group, tactfully mention in the very beginning that this type of behaviour will not be permitted. If you locate him at a later stage, straightaway prevent him from using this tactics.

If possible speak to him in private.

### 6. Member who thinks he knows exactly what is to be done in all cases and considers the conference a waste of time

Encourage other members to comment freely on what he says. Expose him as much as possible to the group. If he makes the slightest move in the direction of creative contribution, recognise it, ask for more advice and generally try to build up a friendly relationship.

**7. Member who attempts to get leader's opinion in all matters and refuses to think for himself**

Refer his question back to the group and then back to him. Do not encourage dependency.

## HANDLING DIFFICULT SITUATION

**1. Conference gets disorderly**

Everyone starts speaking at the same time or gets out of control.

Use silence to attract attention.

If side conversation is going on, direct your eyes to that group and pause.

Tap table gently and direct questions to the offending group.

If everything fails, firmly and tactfully call for order.

**2. Conference loses sight of subject under discussion**

As far as possible this should not happen. If it does happen, summarise what has been said before and ask question to lead to the next relevant step.

Tactfully ask how what is discussed is related to the subject under consideration.

**3. Group is lethargic and does not respond**

Show the group that you are vitally interested in the subject. Make a challenging or provocative statement. Make a dramatic or intentionally exaggerated statement.

**4. Group is self conscious because of the presence of a superior**

Treat him like any other member in the group. Do not let him sit in a special position.

Do not put members in a position where they get embarrassed before a superior.

## QUALITIES OF A GOOD LEADER

**What he should be**

1. He should be a clear, rapid and analytical thinker.

2. He must possess ease of expression in order to ask questions and re-phrase responses.

3. He must be free from prejudices and capable of maintaining an open and unbiased attitude towards members.

4. He must be tactful and sympathetic and must possess enough self-restrain not to dominate the group even whilst expressing his own ideas.

5. He must have a sense of humour so as to drive home a point without hurting others. He must be both an efficient and likeable person; capable of winning confidence and respect.

### What he should do

1. Prepares himself in advance. Gives adequate notice to members. Sends advance literature if necessary. Knows precisely the objective of the conference, goes over the subject, anticipates directions in which discussion will flow, gathers necessary data, etc.

2. Checks to see that physical tools and facilities are provided for viz., display materials, charts, case histories, handouts, as well as proper seating and lighting arrangements.

3. Listens thoughtfully before questioning thereby inculcating the listening habit in other members of the group.

4. Gives out ideas freely and if necessary, vehemently, without being afraid of friendly disagreement. However, he is careful not to dominate the group or monopolise the discussion.

5. Keeps track of time and does not let the conference go on until everybody is exhausted.

6. Talks aloud and with enthusiasm. Avoids nervous (but not expressive) gestures, uses words that are simple and familiar to members and when a point is made, illustrates it, as far as possible.

# Industrial Relations

# 17

Healthy and Harmonious 'Industrial Relations' is an essential prerequisite to 'Human Resource Development'. Industrial relations in a country is intimately connected with the form of its political government, and the objectives of an industrial organisation may vary from purely economic to purely political ends. Industrial societies necessarily create industrial relations, defined as the complex of interrelations among workers, management and the Government. Thus, Industrial relations previously, bipartite, has become tripartite. Dale Yoder defines 'industrial relations' as "a whole field of relationship that exists because of the necessary collaboration of men and women in the employment process of an industry."

## Industrial Relations defined

Broadly speaking, 'industrial relations' means relationship and issues that emerges out of day-to-day working and association of labour and management in the course of running an industry such as:

- Productivity, technological advances, profitability;
- Wages, welfare, service conditions;
- Collective bargaining etc.

And, involving attempts of workable solutions between conflicting interests and harmony.

Industrial relations has also been extended to denote the relations of the Government with employers, workers and their organisation, and the part played by the Government in regulating these relations for the maintenance of industrial development and harmony.

## Industrial Relations System

J.T. Dunlop has given industrial relations, a "system" treatment indicating thereby the possibility of differentiating among different relationships based on peculiar socio-economic conditions. According to him, the term "Industrial Relations" should not be construed as one which denotes the union-management relations operating within the spectrum of industrial peace or conflict. On the other hand, it should be taken as one connected with the larger subject of industrial relations as a whole, in which there are interactions among other groups also and linkage established with the economic and social systems prevailing in society. Thus, the full range of complex interactions among the various groups such as workers and managers, workers trade unions and employers or their organisations together with those interactions linked with the social system as a whole and more particularly with the economic system is referred to as industrial relations system.

The principal groups identifiable in the system and which constitute the structure of industrial relations are as follows:

(1) A hierarchy of employers, managers and their organisations and their representatives or supervisors.

(2) Workers and their organisations and their representatives.

(3) Specialised governmental agencies which are concerned with the workers and their relationships with the employers.

More than the structure of the industrial relations system, the contexts or determinants of the system are of greater importance. The determinant forces can be grouped as follows:

- The technological context of the society,
- The economic or the market constraints which influence the behaviour of the groups, and
- The power context, i.e., the distribution of power among the groups at a particular moment of time.

### Technological Context

It includes:

- The characteristics of the work place, and
- The development of technology.

The characteristics of work place affect the industrial relations climate in an industry which in turn has an impact on the industrial relations system as a whole. For instance, the mining industry has a different technological context as compared to the manufacturing industries. Mining communities have frequently been isolated from important urban areas and create special problems in human relations.

The development of technology affects industrial relations by way of not only disturbing the existing employment patterns but also by determining the size of the work force employed, schemes of rationalisations and automations, for instance, are resisted by workers.

### The Market Context

The market context or the economic factors which greatly influence industrial relations include the competitive position of the industry in the market, the scope of the market as also the size of the enterprise and the lower cost and the capacity of the industry to pay, etc. These factors affect the product market which in turn affect the lower management relationships in the shape of rules and awards etc., which govern the place.

### The Power Context

The policy of the Government, the attitude of the employers, the status of industrial workers, the question of recognition of unions, etc., are all interrelated. The power of Government to direct and control the affairs, the style of management, the degree of unionisation, the extent of membership, political ideologies, etc., exert influence on industrial relations.

The actors in a given context establish rules for work place and the work community, including those governing the contracts among the industrial relations systems. These rules are broadly grouped by Dunlop into three categories, viz.:

- The recruitment and commitment of labour force,
- Compensation and wages,
- Procedures for the settlement of disputes over the application for the existing complex of rules or the new rules.

These rules may be expected to be altered as a consequence of changes in the contexts, the technological, market or social contexts and in the relative status of the actors. The actors who set the rules may be workers and their unions constituting one category employers, managers and their associations having similar interest forming a second category and government is the third category consisting of civil servants concerned with the labour matters.

The rules of the system may be expressed in a variety of forms: the regulations and policies of government hierarchy, the laws of any worker hierarchy; the regulations, decrees, decisions, awards or orders of governmental agencies; collective bargaining agreements; customs and traditions of work place and work community.

### Indian IR

The modern day industrial relations scene in India is largely influenced by the legislative framework. Laws are the expression of a society's intents and purposes in regulating the life of its citizens. However, the grip of statutes is such that in most enterprises the human factor in management is forgotten or ignored.

Legislation concerning industrial relations in any country has to be seen in the light of the social, political and economic history of that land and the impact of contemporary events, both internal and external, that influence the evolution of that society.

Industrial laws in a socialistic welfare country like India are enacted with the purpose of promoting welfare, establishment of industrial harmony and ensuring adequate social security. Industrial law has certainly influenced the organized sector to a large extent. However, a majority of the country's working class is still employed in the unorganised sector, where there is hardly any protection to this weak section and exploitation is the call of the day.

Undoubtedly, psychological and sociological considerations should play an important role in management of human resources. However, as and when the need to take a legal course arises, one needs to understand and appreciate the legal provisions in their true form and spirit in order that justice is done and objectives achieved. It should be well understood that legal provisions are meant to resolve the problems and settle the disputes and not aggravate them or precipitate matters.

Statutory provisions override all other sources of terms and conditions of service whether they be awards, settlements or expressly agreed terms between an employee and employer. In case of difficulty in interpretation of a statute, the benefit of doubt is passed on to the employees since the legislations have a social characteristic. Employers are however free to frame their own rules and regulations or may enter into a settlement with the employees or their unions on various matters. However, such freedom is allowed to be exercised only if the schemes, regulations, settlements etc., are either in conformity with the legal provisions or are more liberal. The sources of terms of employment of employer-employee contract are as follows:

(i) Statutes or Laws of the country.

(ii) Awards given by the courts and tribunals.

(iii) Settlements signed by the employer and the employees under the Industrial Disputes Act, 1947.

(iv) Standing orders if applicable.

(v) Express terms of employment as specified in appointment letters and other related correspondence.

(vi) Customs, usages and practices prevalent in the organisation.

(vii) Implied terms and conditions of employment relationship.

(viii) Rules and regulations framed by the employer for performance of duties and conduct.

Thus, the employer-employee contract for employment is not only governed by the law of contracts but also by various labour legislations under the law of the land, the relationships are determined by the free will of the parties based on respective lawful needs and not by the circumstances.

Changing social ethos gave birth to legislations governing 'employer-employee' relations. As per the modern concept an employer is a body or an agency that offers employment to people in order to meet its own need, while the employee is a person who seeks employment and offers his services and in return satisfies his need of wages. Here the relationship centers around satisfaction of each other's needs and is voluntary in nature.

Thus, the relationship is caused due to the need to satisfy one another and there exists an agreement between the parties which is governed by the principles of the law of contract. Society is dependent to a very large extent on the industrial world, society and in turn the government therefore gets roped into this otherwise bilateral relationship.

While administering the country it becomes essential for the Government to take legislative steps which will lay the foundations of social security against the risks to which citizens are exposed. It is essential to eradicate poverty, unemployment and diseases without which democracy cannot survive on a long-term basis. It will therefore be seen that industrial jurisprudence revolve around social security concepts like maternity, invalidity, employment injuries, unemployment, old age, death, employment security etc.

The social philosophy of the wage, supplies the background for the decision of industrial disputes as to wage structure. A legalistic definition of wage could be, all remunerations capable of being expressed in terms of money, which would, under the terms of contract of employment be payable to a person employed, or for work done in such employment. To pay anything more than the minimum fixed is dependent solely on the collective bargaining, the employer's capacity to pay and industrial and regional norms. Industrial adjudication has played an important role in determination of the structure of wage payments and also fixing basic standards and norms. Broadly speaking, the first principle is that, there is minimum wage which, in any event, must be paid, irrespective of the extent of profits, the financial condition of the establishment or the availability of workmen on lower wages.

The cause of major disputes in India concerns wages, bonus and allowances. As Kudchedkar has pointed out: "Indian IR is vested in terms of profits, wages and dividends to the determinant of social and national interests." Long drawn legal battles and unsettled demands for wages prolonged for years, lead to frustration and low productivity, unrest and strife. Trade Union leaders and employers get busy in satisfying only their own selfish aims without a broader concern for the working class. This is undoubtedly an unhealthy sign.

Government intervention therefore in the form of legislations to regulate the conditions of employment and resolution of conflicts is inevitable. However, a plethora of industrial legislations and ever growing industrial jurisprudence has not only created confusion but also has governed the industrial relations scene in this country. The influence of legislations is of such a magnitude that it has virtually replaced collective bargaining as a technique to settle disputes or resolve grievances. Even in day to day dealings, the employers as well as employees are conditioned almost at every step by the legal framework. The excessive influence of the industrial law on the life of an employer and also the employee, is certainly not a healthy sign. The human side of the relationship process gets forgotten. This perhaps is inevitable in a country where healthy strong unions dedicated to the cause of workmen are rarely seen and the employers exploit the situation of politicized, multiple and weak unions.

The law governing industrial relations is an attempt to mitigate the disequilibrium inherent in any employment relations. The legislation is only a tool to mould the contracts of employment. The adjudication process arises, out of a legislation. The main objective of any industrial adjudication is, therefore, "counterveiling force to counteract the inequalities of bargaining power which is inherent in the employment relationship. It may be noted that Government intervention in the form of compulsory adjudication has significantly contributed to the settlement of a variety of disputes between employers and their employees, but its very success is a failure of collective bargaining which should in the true sense be the normal method of settling industrial disputes. It follows from this, that if the collective bargaining has to gain grounds, compulsory adjudication must diminish. It is far better to leave the management and the trade union to settle their own disputes rather than leave them to third party settlements.

The Industrial relations system revolves around development of harmonious, meaningful and productive relations between the parties.

There can however be no general consensus on the methods of resolving the industrial disputes in a manner that will take care of the social, economic, political and psychological needs of the human beings. Methods acceptable to a party may not be acceptable to another mainly because of ideological reasons.

In order that a proper climate for industrial harmony is created, it is essential that both the parties viz., employers and employees develop an open mind and come together on common platform to resolve conflicts and share areas of mutual concern and interests. In order that this is achieved both the parties must be equal to one another, trust one another and respect each other. Employers will have to develop an open mind and accept the employees as partners of the industry. Employees in turn will also have to acquire right knowledge, strength through unity, matured self-reliant minds which can relate with employees on an equal footing and maturity to accept the employer's problems as their own.

The Constitution of India has affirmed to all people of the country, inter alia, social and economic justice. It is aptly said, "It is the function of an ideal welfare state to give to every citizen the opportunity of earning his living and freedom from fear, especially of economic ruin which can involve physical and even moral ruin."

The First Five Year Plan of the Government of India (Page 572) very aptly describes this entire system: "Peace in industry has a great significance as a force for world peace if we consider the wider implications of the question. The answer to class antagonisms and world conflicts will arrive soon if we succeed in discovering a sound basis for human relations in industry.

Economic progress is also bound up with industrial peace. Industrial relations are, therefore, not a matter between employers and employees alone, but a vital concern of the community which may be expressed in measures for the protection of its larger interests."

According to the National Commission on Labour (p. 53, para 6.36):

> "'Industrial Peace' and 'Industrial Harmony' may have the same meaning; but we are inclined to think that the concept of industrial peace is somewhat negative and restrictive. It emphasises absence of strife and struggle. The concept of industrial harmony is positive and comprehensive and it postulates the existence of understanding, co-operation and a sense of partnership between employers and the employees. That is why we prefer to describe our approach as one in the quest of industrial harmony." Management of Human Resources and the employer-employee relationship are dynamic socio-economic processes. Mutual respect and trust become the basis for any productive, mutually beneficial and harmonious relationship. This is a socio-economic system based on the foundation of collaboration which ultimately results in fulfilment of mutual needs. Like any other relationship this also goes through the alternate stages of conflict-collaboration-conflict and so on. In this dynamic system both the parties are interdependent and therefore they must have an inherent desire for industrial harmony.

# Trade Union and Collective Bargaining

18

Industrial relations in general and trade union policy in particular have tended to become major conditioning factors in Human Resource management. The management in most of the organizations have to work subject to two major constraints, viz., trade union pressure and the laws of the country. A discussion on industrial relations thus remains incomplete without a full-scale consideration of union-management relations and the laws relating to labour relations.

With the growth of the trade union in an organization, the management's role in Industrial Relations undergoes a basic transformation. Without any union, or with a sleeping or inactive trade union, the management could make work rules unilaterally. Now in this respect and also in many matters, the management has lost much of the effective privilege of unilateral decision-making. In the major areas of union concern, e.g., wages, employment, etc., it would deliberately try to share the prerogative of decision-making with the management, either through collective bargaining and its weapons (e.g., strikes, demonstrations etc.) or, where such scope exists, through the forums for joint-consultation and participative management. In other areas, where it may not intervene directly, the management always has to consider any potential union reaction to their decisions. In these fields, the managers may take their decisions on their own, but while doing so they must take into account whether their decisions may contain any irritants which may put off a sizeable section of the workface and may encourage the union to make an issue of it. If adoption of that type of a decision is unavoidable, the management must, in anticipation, think of the measures that have to be taken in case of an objection by the union.

With the growth of the union, the management is also required to take special care in maintaining adequate personnel records, for enabling it to take correct decisions about the workforce, or to support its own actions in the face of the union objection. They also have greater compulsions then to effectively implement the decisions regarding personnel matters, particularly those which appear agreeable to the workers. In addition, top management in general, and Human Resource managers or I.R. managers particularly, have also to understand the nature, strengths and weaknesses of the unions operating in their organization.

The trade union, in effect, is a voluntary organization of the employees to protect and promote the interests of their working lives and to improve their status.

There may be various types of organizing practices of unions. Under the one shop unions, or factory-based or enterprise based unions, the employees are organized on the basis of common employment in a single undertaking. In India, this is the usual mode of organization at the unit-level. However, in Europe and also in North America, most of the unions are organized either at the level of the industry as a whole or at the craft level. In case of industrial unions, there are 'locals' or 'units' which are organized either at the workplace level, or at the level of a locality. For smaller and medium sized concerns, the enterprise based unions usually remain weak due to their small size. However, this deficiency can be reduced if they are organized as industrial unions. In India, there are very few industrial unions. At the level of the entire industry a federation of the enterprise-unions is organized to co-ordinate them, or for the purpose of bargaining with the employers who may prefer to be represented by their associations (e.g., Indian Jute Mills Association, Indian Tea Association, etc.) in matters in which they prefer to have a combined policy. At the national level, the individual trade unions have their national trade union centres (e.g., INTUC, AITUC, CITU or HMS in India, AFL - CIO in U.S.A. TUC in U.K., SOHYO in Japan, etc.). in our country, there are about seven major national trade union centres, each competing with the other. Each of them is associated with one political party or the other. Their existence is an important factor behind the problems of multiple unionism and trade union rivalry at the enterprise level.

In between the national trade union centres and the individual trade unions, there are state units or zonal units of the particular national or regional industrial federations at the level of the industry. Like the enterprise-level, at the industry-level also, there are multiple organizations according to the affiliations to particular national centres. For understanding the dynamics of trade union movement and the expected trade union policy in his enterprise, a Human Resource manager (or manager of industrial relations) must understand these political moorings and affiliation patterns. In addition to the enterprise-unions or industrial-unions, there are two other types of the trade union organizational system, viz., 'craft unions' and 'general unions'. In the craft union, the membership is open only to the employees belonging to a particular craft or occupational group. The units of Ahmedabad Textile Labour Association (T.L.A.) are organized according to the craft unionism. There are unions for weavers, spinners, etc., which are all combined and co-ordinated by T.L.A. Unions of employees which organize only specific occupational groups, e.g., All India Station Masters Union, Indian Airlines Pilots Guild, etc., also may be described as essentially craft unions.

'General Unions' are rarely seen in India, although in U.K. and also in some underdeveloped countries like Ceylon and Thailand there are many such unions. In U.K., there are many strong 'general unions', i.e., National Union of General and Municipal Workers, Transport and General Workers Union etc., which organize workers belonging to several industries and occupational groups. In India, these unions are seen in some industrial centres and industrial estates, where most of the enterprises being small in size, the development of enterprise-level or industrial unions are difficult. Adityapur Workers' Union (INTUC) and Adityapur Industrial Mazdoor Union (CITU) operating in Adityapur Industrial Area near Jamshedpur may be cited as instances of general unions, as their membership is open to any industrial worker working in Adityapur industrial area, irrespective of the enterprise or the industry to which he may belong.

Although the management should not interfere with the choice of the type or structure of the union in their particular organization and should leave the matter entirely to the workers, it may be worthwhile to consider the relative advantages and problems of the particular types of trade unions from the point of view of the collective bargaining and better union-management relations. Dealing with craft unions may be relatively more difficult for the management, as that may create difficulties of uniform scales of pay and conditions of service for employees of the same organization irrespective of their occupational distinctions. From this point of view, enterprise-unions or industrial-unions may be better. There would be some difficulty in dealing with the 'general unions' as well, because their leaders, bargaining on behalf of the workers of several undertakings in different industries, may not appreciate the special situations in a particular industry or undertaking.

## Collective Bargaining

Collective Bargaining refers to a process of negotiations, threats, counter-threats and related pressure-tactics adopted by the employers and the organized workers represented by their union in order to determine the terms and conditions of employment. The essential thing about the collective bargaining is the fact that it is an instrument of joint rule-making in an economic organization, as distinct from unilateral rule-making or rule-making by a third party. The ultimate end of collective bargaining is to reach some settlement acceptable to both the parties involved in labour-management relations, although each of them tries to impose its own terms upon the other through pressure tactics and negotiations.

The significant role of collective bargaining is widely accepted today. It has a very significant contribution in improving the labour-management relations and in ensuring industrial harmony. The negotiations for collective bargaining require joint sessions of the representatives of labour and management.

These help a lot in better understanding of each other's point of view as well as problems. Through discussions and interactions, both the parties learn more about others and often misunderstandings may be removed. Although all major differences may not be always sorted out, collective bargaining helps in easing out many minor differences and there are plenty of instances in which it helped to settle even major disputes without any work-stoppage or outside intervention. Accordingly, its role in conflict resolution is very significant.

## Developing a Bargaining Relationship

One of the earliest steps in collective bargaining system in an organization is the development of a regular and systematic procedure for bargaining. The first question in this connection for the management is to decide who should be accepted as the representatives of workers for this purpose. The next question is what should be the level of bargaining, i.e., whether bargaining should be only at the enterprise level, or should there be bargains at the industrial and the national levels, as well as at the shop-floor or the departmental levels. The third question is what should be the scope and coverage of issues under collective bargaining.

## Choice of the Bargaining Agent or the Representative Union

In those organizations in which there is a single trade union the answer to the first question is obvious in the collective bargains, the workers would be represented only by the union. However, the matter becomes complicated in organizations in which there are several unions, each claiming the exclusive right to represent all the workers including the non-members. The management then has a problem in deciding whom to accept as the bargaining agent. And this is very crucial decision. If the management wilfully, or by mistake, chooses a union which actually does not command majority support among the workers, collective agreements signed with it may not carry much weight and the unrecognized union or unions may disrupt work, or cause work-stoppages on the ground of the recognition itself, or against the settlement. If, however, the decision is correctly made, the representative union on account of its majority support, or by virtue of being the single largest union, may carry the majority of workers in favour of the settlements accepted by it in spite of the hue and cry made by the smaller unions. So the management, in this issue, should be guided not by its own preferences or views as to who should represent the workers, but must objectively judge which union can deliver the goods, i.e., can be instrumental in getting the acceptance of the collective settlements by the majority of the workers.

For identifying the union or the bargaining agent which can meet this criterion, the management may choose one of the several options available to it, viz.: (a) selection of the representative union by secret ballot, or (b) selection through verification of membership by some

Government agency, (c) bargaining with a joint committee of all the major unions, (d) bargaining with a negotiating committee in which different unions would be represented in proportion of their verified membership, (e) bargaining with a negotiating committee which consists of elected representative of every department of the organization selected by secret ballot irrespective of their union-allegiance.

The secret ballot is widely used and sanctioned by law in many countries, e.g., the United States, West Germany, Phillippines, etc. India, most of the central trade union organizations, viz., AITUC, HMS, UTUC, CITU, etc., supported this method of determining the representative union, although another central organization, i.e., INTUC, opposed it. The National Commission on Labour in its Report gave it partial support. It preferred to leave the determination of the representative union to the proposed Industrial Relations Commission, which might use either secret ballot or the verification procedure for that purpose. The method is democratic and reduces the scope of manipulation by the Government, or the employers, in favour of a union which may be truly representative.

Supporters of membership verification by either the Government or an autonomous statutory, on the other hand, criticize the secret ballot as a mechanism which would expose the workers to political issues which may not be relevant for trade union representation in an enterprise or industry. Moreover, they hold that the payment of regular membership subscriptions to a particular union itself is a vote in favour of that union, which in fact indicates a worker's preference for it over the others. The opponents, however, point out that the employers, or a rich group of people, or a political party supporting a minority union may pay subscriptions out of their own pockets on behalf of the apathetic workers, or workers who do not support the particular union, in order to unduly influence the process of verification. It may be difficult for a genuine trade union enjoying the support of majority of the poor workers to complete with it on this basis.

A way out for this problem is to leave the right to bargain on behalf of the employees to bargaining committee or negotiating committee, in which all the unions may be represented according to the total unionized workforce commanded by them. These proportions may be determined by verification of the dues-paying members over a certain minimum period of time. The verification should be done by an independent statutory authority, and not by the Labour Department of the Government. This method would be free from the difficulties of secret ballot, or verification of membership for the choice of a single bargaining agent, and would give some voice to the relatively large unions, which may not be in a position to command the largest number of votes or membership, but have got significant support. This would also be better than the practice of negotiations through a Joint Committee of different unions, which has been followed in several Indian industries having multiple unions in the course of collective bargaining. In situations of crisis, or extraordinary occasions like that of a wage-dispute or major retrenchment, different unions may speak together through a Joint-Committee. But on all occasions, such unity of voice of the rival unions may not be possible and they may refuse to come to the same bargaining table on the same side. The attempt to form the Joint Committee may be particularly opposed by the largest or the recognized union (if there is one) which may claim the right to speak on behalf of all the employees of the undertaking or the industry.

However, the method suggested above (i.e., constitution of a bargaining committee on the proportional strength of the unions) should be tried out only when the largest union is still a minority union, and there are other strong rivals to it. If the secret ballot or verification conducted by an independent statutory authority indicates that any particular union has got an absolute majority of eligible employees, it should be given recognition as the 'Sole Bargaining Agent'. The other unions then may be given the right to represent their member's grievances.

### Level of Bargaining

Collective bargaining is possible at different levels, viz., at the level of enterprise, at the level of the entire industry in the country (i.e., national industrial level) or at the level of the industry at a particular region (i.e., regional-industry level). From the point of view of an individual establishment, an advantage of the enterprise-level bargaining lies in the possibility of a settlement exactly tailored to the conditions of the concern, e.g., its capacity to pay, its market conditions and objectives, etc. However, for relatively smaller or medium sized units, it may be difficult to achieve satisfactory bargaining results, if the workers are represented by a strong industrial union or federation. Again, if the bargaining is characterized by the presence, or influence of the officials of the Government, the small or medium sized employers may often find it difficult to gather sufficient facts and data in support of their stand. In fact, now-a-days in many industrial disputes covering large number of units in an industry, Ministers of the State or the Central Government intervene directly. In such bargaining, they prefer settlements applicable to the entire industry, or to the industry of a particular region. This naturally requires the employers to be represented collectively by their association instead of each company bargaining individually with the trade unions. However, in the disputes which are localized in particular industrial units or business organizations (e.g., the disputes on the quantum of bonus in individual organizations which characterize the pre-Puja or pre-Diwali months in many states), the bargaining may be conducted at the enterprise level.

As regards the coverage of issues of collective bargaining, much management may prefer to bargain only on the specific issues (e.g., wage-increase, or bonus, or seniority, promotion, etc.) which are raised by the trade union as demands. It is, however advantageous both to the management as well as to the trade unions to use the occasion of collective bargaining to cover as many issues of interest to both parties as possible. A wide coverage of issues in bargaining and in the resulting collective agreements or settlements help in preventing many potential sources of friction which may not come to the surface at a particular time, but may create disputes later on. In addition to the interest-centred issues (e.g., wages, bonus, recruitment, retrenchment, etc.), it is desirable to cover at the earliest bargaining opportunity several other issues, like grievance procedure, procedures of collective bargaining, union security clauses like union-shop, closed shop, etc., and issues of common interest like improvement of productivity, worker's participation in management, changes in technology of production, etc., wherever these are not covered by earlier agreements, or whenever future frictions of any of these issues is anticipated.

Negotiations in the course of collective bargaining, as we have already indicated, ultimately aim at reaching some settlement or collective agreement, in which both the parties want to get as much of their respective positions formally accepted by the other party, such negotiations often are long and tedious and require a good deal of skill, knowledge and fact on both sides.

### Preparation for the Negotiation

Before the negotiation starts, each side in collective bargaining tries to prepare its own case as convincingly as possible with the necessary facts and evidence, and also seeks to determine the maximum concessions it can give to the other side, if necessary, and the maximum concessions to be expected from the other side. These require thorough understanding of the factors which have bearings on the collective bargaining process and its outcome. Broadly speaking, the respective stands taken by the employers and the union would depend on the anticipated costs of the possible work stoppage (due to strikes and lock-outs) for itself and for the other side, the higher the expected costs of work stoppage to itself, the greater would be the concessions to be offered. On the other hand, the higher the expected costs to the other side, the stiffer would be its attitude to the other side's viewpoint. In the section on the determinants of the fighting power of each side in a strike, we would analyze these costs of strikes in details. Here we discuss other factors which should be considered by the parties in determining their own bargaining strategies before the negotiation starts.

Briefly speaking, in addition to the costs of work-stoppage, these other factors depend greatly on the analysis of (a) the market context, (b) the financial context, and (c) the technological context in which the industry or the organization operates. In general, these are the economic determinants of collective bargaining. Besides these, there are some socio-political determinants as well, viz., the power context and the expected Government policy about the dispute. For the market context, both sides should try to understand the existing state of the market for the product or service of the organization and the cyclical or other changes of the business expected in near future. In a highly competitive market, the employers should try to avoid work-stoppage even by granting relatively greater concessions, particularly when the demand for its product is good. It should also judge the price elasticity of demand for its products, because that would indicate the extent to which any possible increase in the price necessitated by concessions to the workers would affect the demand. In a monopoly situation, or in those cases of monopolistic competition where the product image is such as to preclude any near substitute, the employers may adopt a stiffer attitude, as the work-stoppage would not affect them much. However, if for other reasons (mainly non-economic) it desires to adopt a lenient position, its capacity to be lenients is also greater than that of a producer in a highly competitive market. Similarly, while deciding on its bargaining strategy the employers may adopt a more lenient attitude during a boom, than during a recession. So the expected changes in the business cycle in near future also should be analyzed and anticipated carefully before collective bargaining starts. It is also necessary to analyze the relevant labour-market situations in terms of availability of labour, wages in other concerns and other details.

The employers, while determining its own bargaining strategy, also carefully consider their financial capacity to pay, as reflected in the expected sales-incomes, its own liquid cash position, the prospects of bank-credit, the expected profits in future, the minimum rate of return on equity-capital, needs of reinvestment and the total productivity of the unit concerned. They should also carefully anticipate the possible impact of the industrial relations — both in terms of a settlement and show-down on the supply of external finances. They should also carefully work out the technological implications in terms of maintenance of the idle plant in case of a work-stoppage, expected impact of the settlement on the technological operation of the company and so on. Among the non-economic factors, the management should anticipate the possible reactions of the Board of Directors and the Annual General Meeting of the shareholders to their stands in the course of collective bargaining, resulting either in a showdown, or a settlement. Such anticipations naturally would depend on the power equations within the organization — whether the management (including its leader, i.e., the Chairman or the Managing Director) can carry the Board and the shareholders with it, or not. The management also must take into account the power equations among the workers and within the Union. They should judge the extent to which the Union leaders can carry the Union itself and the workers at large to support any settlement that it may reach with the management. In addition to all these, the management must carefully think about the Government's industrial relations policy, the national wage policy, the economic situation in general and the inflationary context in particular, for anticipating what would be the possible reaction of the Government in this industrial dispute — whether it would remain apathetic or neutral, or would actively intervene to force a settlement. In the latter case, it should also judge whether the Government's position would tilt more in favour of the management or the labour.

Naturally for making judgements on such questions, the management must have sufficient data, as well as sources of information on all these matters. Prior to any collective bargaining, the management must ensure that it has all these relevant details, some of these facts, particularly those relating to its own personnel, may be obtained from the analysis of the existing and past personnel records. Others are to be obtained from different sources, e.g., materials published by the Government or official agencies (like commissions, tribunals, etc.), academic institutions, business organizations and individuals, direct enquiries with employers, associations and Chambers of Commerce, direct enquiries with other organization, etc.

## Bargaining Procedures and Strategies

The collective bargaining process, in additon to negotiations for reducing the differences in the viewpoints of the management and labour, also depends a good deal on mutual brow-beating, threats and counter-threats for inducing the other party to accept its own terms. If the negotiations break down, the parties may resort to work-stoppage in the form of strikes by labour, or lock-outs by the management. Besides, the workers also make use of other tactics, e.g., demonstrations, gheraos, go-slow, tool-down strike, etc., for pressurizing the management to accept their points of view. The management, in its turn, uses some other pressure tactics before declaring a lock-out, e.g., strict enforcement of disciplinary measures, transfer of leading union personnel from their departments or plants, circulars and notices explaining their views to the rank and file of workers, newspaper advertisements for creating favourable public opinion and so on. All these pressure tactics (including strikes and lock-outs) used by either side should be considered as inherent parts of the collective bargaining process. Opening the negotiations is the first step in the bargaining process. This appears to be a simple and formal matter, but is by no means easy or unimportant. In fact, to some extent, the hostility of the union representatives, particularly those belonging to the lower ranks can be somewhat softened by a cordial reception, indicating the willingness of the management side to be friendly. A small dose of humour may ease the stiffness of the initial interaction but that should not be overdone, or be artificial.

The first session should be utilized for getting clarifications and details of the supporting materials from the opposite side to understand what they actually want.

The next important step, which should be taken both between the sessions and also during the second session, is the analysis of the proposals and careful examination of their implications by each side. Part of this session may be devoted to drawing attention of the other side to the implications of their stands for the entire organization, or its workforce as a whole. For its own judgement, each side at this stage would try to identify both from the documents circulated as well as from the clarifications issued during the sessions, the hardcore demands of the other side on which they may offer fight. These items should be isolated from the less important items on which the other side would not be much fastidious. Particularly from the management point of view, identification of the hard-core demands of the union and examination of their implications for the company are crucial for correct formulation of their own bargaining strategy.

The third step, which in effect, almost consists of the essence of the actual bargaining, is the attempt to resolve the differences between the proposals of the two sides, this stage witnesses most of the gives-and-takes as well as bluffs, threats and counter-threats, which are used as pressure tactics during the sessions. However, if the negotiations at this stage fail to resolve the differences and a deadlock is reached, more severe pressures are applied in the fourth stage. From the labour side, the pressures at this stage may take the form of 'gheraos' or 'strikes backed by gate-picketing' and, in the case of consumer items, call to the public for boycotting the products of the company. From the management side, their response to the pressure-tactics at this stage may be a lock-out which in effect, is work-stoppage forced by the employers. Sometimes, this stage of direct confrontation is followed by a return to the bargaining table, when both sides have sobered down after experiencing the costs of work-stoppage or tactics of confrontation. But in some other occasions, when the parties are in no mood to resume negotiations, the issues may be referred by the Government to conciliation and failing that to adjudication by a Labour Court, or Industrial

Tribunal. Sometimes, the parties instead of going for adjudication may prefer to refer the dispute to the arbitration of an arbitrator or a panel of arbitration, jointly selected by them by mutual agreement. Under the Industrial Disputes Act, 1947, the concerned Government, whether state or central, may compulsorily refer any industrial dispute to a Board of Conciliation, or to a Labour Court, or an Appropriate Tribunal. However, if the dispute relates to a public utility service, reference of dispute to conciliation or arbitration is obligatory for the Government. The Government has also to make, such a reference to conciliation, or arbitration, if both the parties in the dispute demand in writing and if they represent the majority in each side. Strikes and lock-outs are prohibited during the pendency of conciliation or arbitration proceedings, or the proceedings of adjudication before a Labour Court, Tribunal or National Tribunal and seven days thereafter in case of the conciliation and arbitration and two months thereafter in the case of adjudication.

### Determinants of the Fighting Powers of the Union and the Management: An exercise in the estimation of the expected duration of work stoppage

The process of collective bargaining as well as its outcome depend a good deal on the actual fighting powers of the parties concerned and also on their respective estimates of the fighting powers of the opposite side. These fighting powers mainly mean the capacity of a party in collective bargaining to force a work stoppage (in the form of a strike by the workers, or lock-out by the management) and to sustain it for the required duration till the other party is forced to mellow down. The fighting power in collective bargaining depends mainly on the estimated cost of the work stoppage (strike or lock-out) to the party concerned and also on its estimate of the other party's costs arising out of the stoppage. To the employers, the cost of the work-stoppage, other things remaining the same, would be great if the demand for their products or their service in the market is very favourable, but competition is so keen that a work stoppage may cause good deal of transfer of the demand to the competitors. It would be still higher, if the inventory of the product is small or the nature of the product is such as to exclude the possibility of inventory holding. The cost of work stoppage also depends on the elasticity of substitution of the striking employees by outsiders or new recruits. If they cannot be substituted by others, or if the production in the plant stopped by the strike cannot be transfered to another plant under the same organisation, the cost of the work stoppage would be considerable for the employers. The financial conditions and requirements of the organization also affect the costs of work-stoppage. If it requires continuous flow of funds from the stock-exchange, and if its cash-flow position is such as to require repeated credits from the banks, a long drawn-out work stoppage is likely to damage the interests of the organization. Naturally that would weigh heavily against the fighting power of the management. The union's fighting power on the other hand depends mainly on the size of its strike-fund and its financial position in general, the ability of the members to borrow from different sources during the strike, the extent of availability of other assets (liquid as well as non-liquid) to them and their ability to collect donations from sympathisers, or earn additional incomes from odd jobs. If these factors, are unfavourable, the costs of strike to the members would be very high and, to that extent, the union's fighting power will be rather low. It would then be unable to sustain a long-drawn strike and may have to tone down its demands or to accept even unfavourable terms. If the union cannot read the implications of its low fighting power, at times the workers themselves may return to work disregarding the strike, which would then fizzle out.

### The Collective Agreement

The settlement which the union and the management ultimately reach through collective bargaining is usually recorded in a document signed by the representatives of both sides. This is known as Collective Agreement. The Collective Agreement may often be fairly long and complicated document. It usually contains between 20 to 30 clauses or sections. The Agreement determines not only the terms and conditions of service, e.g., wages, hours of work, etc., but also indicates the arrangements for distribution of benefits to the employees. It also contains clauses incorporating the agreed decisions of the management and the union on issues of the dispute between the two sides in addition to those relating to the terms and conditions of work. It often includes clauses which affirm the prerogatives of the management. In many cases, the union also ensures the incorporation or certain clauses which indicate its right and privileges, e.g., provision of an office room in the premises of the organisation and notice board to display the notices of the union, the right to collect subscriptions from the members at the premises and the gate, right to bargain with the management, etc. In some cases the strongest of the several unions demands and gets incorporated into the Agreement a clause indicating the management's recognition of it as the sole bargaining agent. In many countries, the unions also get the 'check-off', i.e., privilege of collection of the union-dues from its members by the management through deducting it from the wages and salaries for handing them over to the union. All such clauses of the Collective Agreement dealing with the rights and privileges of the union, are known as 'union security clauses'. In addition many Agreements also incorporate clauses regulating the procedures of union-management relations and grievance procedures. Although not done always, it is better to definitely state the duration of the Agreement in one of its clauses.

### Legal Frame of Labour Management Relations in India

In India, there are several laws providing the framework of labour-management relations at the establisment level. In the industries, this is regulated by Industrial Disputes Act, 1947, Industrial Employment (Standing Orders) Act, 1946 and the Indian Trade Union Act, 1926. In 1978, a comprehensive Industrial Relations Bill was presented before the Lok Sabha for regulating different aspects of labour-management relations by incorporating provisions relating to the items covered by the three separate Acts and many other issues in a single piece of legislation. However, due to the resistance to certain provisions of the Act separately by the employers and the trade unions, the Government did not force its passage. After the dissolution of Lok Sabha in August, 1979, this bill lapsed automatically. Thus, the labour-management relations in this country are still basically bound within the framework of the three separate Acts as mentioned.

## OUTLINE OF INDUSTRIAL RELATIONS LEGISLATIONS

### Industrial Disputes Act

In this Act, Industry means any systematic activity carried on by cooperation between an employer and his workman for the production, supply or distribution of goods or services with a view to satisfy human wants or wishes, whether or not any capital has been invested for such activity or such activity is carried on with profit-motive (Industrial Disputes Amendment Act, 1982). This definition, however, explicitly excludes hospitals, educational research institutions, scientific or training institute, activities conducted by cooperative societies and khadi and village industries from its scope. Prior to the 1982 Amendment of the Act, the term Industry covered any business, trade, undertaking, manufacturing or calling of employers including any service, employment handicraft or industrial occupation of the workmen. According to a judgment by the Supreme Court in 1978, delivered in Bangalore Water Supply vs. Rajappa Cas, it was held that the meaning was not to be confined to organisations with profit motive only. Hospitals, charitable institutions, educational organisations etc., were considered as industries for the purpose of this Act, provided they carried on systematic activity organised by cooperation between employers and employees for production and distribution of goods and services calculated to satisfy wants or wishes, other than religious or spiritual. The 1982 amendment of the Act, while generally adopting the basic concept of industry as enunciated by the Supreme Court in its judgment in the above mentioned case, deliberately excluded the categories mentioned above from the meaning of the term Industry.

The industrial dispute in this Act means any dispute or difference between employers and workmen engaged in an industry which is connected with the employment or non-employment, or the terms and conditions of employment, or with the conditions of labour of workmen, or those of any person in which workmen as class are interested. The term 'Workman' also has a very wide coverage in this Act and refers to any person, including an apprentice, employed in any industry to do any skilled or unskilled, manual, supervisory, technical, or clerical work for reward. However, this term excludes persons employed mainly in managerial or administrative capacity and those working in supervisory capacity, but drawing a salary or wages more than Rs. 1600 per month. It also excludes persons governed by the Army Act, Air Force Act, Navy Act or persons employed in police service or prisons.

Under this Act, the industrial disputes may be settled by any one or other ways from the following, viz., (a) settlement between parties among themselves when it is recorded as an agreement and copies thereof are sent to the authorities specified, (b) settlement arrived in the course of conciliation proceedings, (c) award by the adjudicator in disputes referred by the Government to the machinery set up under this Act, or (d) award by the arbitrator selected by voluntary consent of the parties in the dispute. The settlements in the form of collective agreements through negotiations between the employers and workmen are binding on the parties to the agreement. But a settlement arrived in the course of conciliation proceedings, or an award of a Labour Court, Tribunal or National Tribunal set up under this Act, is binding on all parties to the industrial dispute and also on the employer, his heirs, successors or assigns in respect of the establishment concerned and on all workmen employed in the establisment concerned. In the event of the parties in industrial dispute failing to reach a settlement among themselves, the Government has been given the power to refer the dispute to conciliation by a Conciliation Officer, or a Board of Conciliation. The officer or the Board would bring the employers and the representatives of the workmen together and try to induce them to reach a settlement. It is obligatory on the part of Government to refer any dispute in a public utility service to conciliation or to adjudication by a Labour Court, Tribunal. On failure of conciliation or if both the sides in an industrial dispute so desire, or if the Government considers it so desirable in the public interest, a dispute may be referred to adjudication by any of the three types of adjudication machinery set under the Act, viz., the Labour Court or a National Tribunal, the Tribunal. The Labour Courts have jurisdiction over disputes on orders passed by the employers under the standing orders of the establishment, the application and interpretation of these standing orders, discharge or dismissals and reinstatements, legality or otherwise of a strike or lock-out, withdrawal of any customary concessions or privileges, etc. The matters under the jurisdiction of the Industrial Tribunals include wages, allowances, bonus, hours of work, leave, holiday, shift working, rules of discipline, rationalisation, retrenchment of workmen, closure of the establishment, etc. The National Tribunal can adjudicate over the industrial disputes involving questions of national importance, or those affecting industrial units situated in more than one state.

The Act also provides for voluntary arbitration in an industrial dispute, if both the sides want to refer the same to an Arbitrator chosen by mutual consent. It also prohibits strikes or lock-outs during the pendency of conciliation, arbitration, or adjudication proceedings or for specified number of days following it (as has been noted earlier).

The Industrial Disputes Act has provided for the machinery for regulating the day-to-day labour-management relations as well. In all industrial undertakings, employing 100 workmen or more, the Government may require the employers to constitute a Works Committee consisting of the representatives of employers and workmen. The Works Committee would "promote measures for securing and preserving amity and good relations between the employers and the workman" and, to that end, would comment upon matters of their common interest and would also endeavour to compose differences of opinion in respect of such matters. The Industrial Disputes Act also provides for payment of compensation to the workmen in the case of any retrenchment and lay-off. The retrenched workmen is to be given one month's notice in writing, or in lieu of that, wages for the period of notice and a compensation which shall be equivalent to fifteen day's average pay for every completed years of service, or any part thereof, in excess of six months, provided he was in continuous service in that industrial establishment for not less than one year. Similarly, a workman, who completed not less than one year's continuous service, is to be paid a compensation for lay-off which would be equivalent to fifty per cent of the total of his basic wages and dearness allowance, which would have been payable if he had not been laid off.

Under the 1982 Amendment of the Industrial Disputes Act, certain activities on the part of the employers and employees have been declared as "Unfair Labour Practices" and punishable under law. The important Unfair Labour Practices on the part of the employers are the following: to interfere with, restrain from or coerce workmen in the exercise of their right to organise, to dominate, interfere with or contribute support, financial or otherwise to any trade union, to establish employer sponsored trade unions of workmen, to encourage or discourage membership in any trade union, to discharge or dismiss workmen for taking part in any strike (other than illegal strike), or by way of victimisation, or for patiently false reasons, or in the utter disregard of natural justice in the conduct of domestic enquiry, to transfer a workman mala fide from one place to another place, failure to implement award, settlement or agreement or to indulge in acts of force or violence.

For the trade unions or the workmen the following are described as Unfair Labour Practice: to advise or actually support any illegal strike, to coerce workmen to join a trade union or to refrain from joining a trade union, to stage, encourage or instigate such forms of coercive actions as wilful go-slow, 'gherao' of any member of the managerial or other staff, to indulge in acts of force or violence etc.

Under the Industrial Employment (Standard Orders) Act, every industrial establishment (as defined under Payment of Wages Act, 1936, or Factories Act, 1948, a railway as defined under Indian Railway Act, 1890, or the establishment of a person who employs workmen for fulfilling a contract with an industrial establishment) employing 100 or more workmen is required to frame standing orders defining conditions of employment of its draft of the standing orders is to be submitted by the management to the certifying officer appointed by the Government — State or Central, as the case may be. On receipt of the drafts, the certifying officer forwards a copy to the trade union (or if there is no trade union, to the workmen together by publishing a notice) asking for objections, if any, to be submitted to him within 15 days from the receipt of the notice and the draft. After giving the employer and the trade union or the representatives of workmen, an opportunity of being heard, the certifying officer certifies the standing orders after making the required modifications in the draft. This Act, therefore, provides an important instrument of regulating the conditions of employment by standing orders, in the framing of which the employers and also the workmen are given the opportunity to participate. Although the Industrial Disputes Act, Industrial Employment (Standing Orders) Act, Minimum Wages Act, Employees State Insurance Act and several other legislations enacted by the Parliament of India provide for some role or say by the Trade Union in the statutory bodies or processes created under these Acts, as yet no Central Legislation has been passed for regulating the recognition of trade union by the employers. The Industrial Relations Bill, 1978, contained some provisions in respect of this, but lapsed with the dissolution of the sixth Lok Sabha. Accordingly, the main legislation governing working of the Trade Unions is still the Indian Trade Union Act, 1926. Under this Act, any seven or more members of a union can apply to the registrar of Trade Unions appointed by the Government for each state for the registration of that Trade Union under this Act. Every such application is to be accompanied by rules of the Trade Union containing its name, objectives, purposes for which the general funds of the Union can be spent, conditions of its membership, procedure and conditions for the appointment or removal of the executive committee or other officers of the union and certain other prescribed matters. The Act gives the registered Trade Union a legal and corporate status and also immunity to its officers and members from the charges of criminal conspiracy for agreement of its members in furtherance of the objectives of the union. No civil suit is also maintainable in any court of law against the registered Trade Union, or its officers or members for acts done in furtherance of its objectives. The auditing of the funds of the registered Union is compulsory and the Act provides for the specific objects for which the general funds of a registered Union can be spent. It also permits the creation of a fund for civil or political interests of its members, but the contributions to it are purely voluntary.

# Labour Welfare

# 19

The Constitution of India not only guarantees some of the fundamental rights to its citizens but also has embodied directive principles of state policy for the achievement of a Social order based on Justice, Liberty, Equality and Fraternity.

It is the function of the welfare of the people (Article 38) to direct its policy that the citizens have the right to an adequate means of livelihood, that the ownership and control of the material resources of the community are so distributed as best to subserve the common good; that the operation of the economic system does not result in the concentration of wealth and means of production of common detriment; that the health and strength of the workers and tender age of children are not forced by economic necessity to enter a vocation unsuited to their age or strength and that the children and youth are protected against exploitation and against moral or material abandonment (Article 39).

Article 41: "The state shall, within the limits of its economic capacity and development, make effective provision for securing the right to work, to education, and to public assistance in cases of unemployment, old-age, sickness, and disablement and in other cases of underserved want." Section 42: "The state shall make provision for securing just and humane conditions of work and for maternity relief." Article 43: "The state shall endeavour to secure, by suitable legislation or economic organisation or in any other way, to all workers—work, a wage, conditions of work ensuring a decent standard of life and full enjoyment of leisure and social and cultural opportunities."

The National Commission on labour has summed up the National Labour Policy in the year 1969 as follows:

(1) Recognition of the state as a custodian of the interests of the community and as a catalyst of 'change' in Welfare Programmes.
(2) Recognition of the rights of worker to peaceful direct action if the justice is denied to them.
(3) Encouragement to bilateral settlements through collective bargaining or voluntary arbitration.
(4) Intervention by the state in favour of the weaker party to ensure fair treatment to all concerned.
(5) State's primary responsibility is to maintain industrial peace and harmony.
(6) Evolving partnership between employer and employees in a constructive manner so that the satisfaction of the economic needs of the community is promoted in the best possible manner.
(7) Ensuring fair wage standards and provision of social security.
(8) Co-operation for increasing the production and productivity.
(9) Adequate enforcement of legislation.
(10) Enhancing the status of the worker in industry.
(11) Tripartite consultations.

**The ILO report refers to labour welfare as**

"Such services, facilities and amenities as may be established in or in the vicinity of undertakings to enable the persons employed in them to perform their work in healthy, congenial surroundings and provided with amenities conducive to good health and high morale."

According to the committee on labour welfare, welfare services should mean: "such services, facilities, and amenities as adequate canteens, rest and recreation facilities, sanitary and medical facilities, arrangements for travel to and from the place of work, and for the accommodations of workers employed at a distance from their homes; and such other services, amenities and facilities, including social security measures, as contribute to the conditions under which workers are employed."

The Committee of Experts on Welfare Facilities for Industrial Workers convened by ILO (in 1963) included the following items under the term 'labour welfare':

A. Welfare and Amenities within the Precincts of the Establishment:

1. Latrines and Urinals.
2. Washing and bathing facilities.
3. Creches.
4. Rest shelters and canteens.
5. Arrangements for drinking water.
6. Health services, including occupational safety.
7. Arrangement for prevention of fatigue.
8. Administrative arrangements for the welfare of employees.
9. Uniform and protective clothings.
10. Shift allowance.

B. Welfare Outside the Establishment:

1. Maternity benefit.
2. Social insurance measures (including gratuity, pension, provident fund and rehabilitation).
3. Benevolent funds.
4. Medical facilities (including programmes for physical fitness and efficiency, family planning and child welfare).
5. Education facilities.
6. Housing facilities.
7. Recreation facilities (including sports, cultural activities, library, reading rooms).
8. Holiday homes and leave travel facilities.
9. Workers' co-operatives, including consumers' co-operative stores, fair price shops, and co-operative credit and thrift societies.
10. Vocational training for dependents of workers.
11. Other programmes for the welfare of women, youth and children.
12. Transport to and from the place of work.

In India, the need for labour welfare was strongly felt by the Royal Commission on labour as far back as in 1931, primarily because of a lack of commitment to industrial work among factory workers and the harsh treatment they received from their employers. The need for labour welfare arises from the very nature of the industrial system, which is characterised by two basic factors: one, the conditions under which work is carried on are not congenial for health; and second, when a labourer joins an industry, he has to work in an entire strange atmosphere, many times, overtime, which create problems of adjustment. Hence the need for provision of welfare services within the premises of the Factory, Mine or Plantations.

Employers in India are statutorily required to supply various labour welfare amenities under different labour laws. These amenities have been statutorily provided under the Factories Act, 1948; the Plantations Act, 1951; the Mines Act, 1952; the Motor Transport Workers Act, 1961; the Contract Labour (Regulation and Abolition) Act, 1970; and the Inter-State Migrant Workmen (Regulation of Employment and Conditions of Service) Act, 1979.

These have been given below:

### The Factories Act, 1948

It provides for:

(i) Washing facilities;

(ii) Facilities for storing and drying clothing;

(iii) Facilities for occasional rest for workers who are obliged to work standing;

(iv) First-aid boxes or cupboards, one for every 150 workers — and the ambulance facility, if there are more than 500 workers;

(v) Canteens, if there are more than 250 workers;

(vi) Shelters, rest-rooms and lunch-rooms, if over 150 workers are employed;

(vii) Creche, if 30 or more women workers are employed;

(viii) Welfare Officer, if 500 or more workers are employed.

### The Plantations Act, 1951

It makes provisions for:

(i) A canteen, if employing 150 or more workers;

(ii) Creche, if employing 50 or more women workers;

(iii) Recreational facilities for workers and their children;

(iv) Educational arrangements on the estates for the children of workers, if there are 25 workers' children between the age of 6 and 12;

(v) Housing facilities for every worker and his family residing on the plantation, in accordance with the prescribed standard laid down by state government;

(vi) Medical aid to workers and their families; sickness and maternity allowance;

(vii) Making available to workers such number and type of umbrellas, blankets, raincoats, or other like amenities for their protection against rain or cold, as prescribed by the state government;

(viii) Welfare Officer, if 300 or more workers are employed.

### The Mines Act, 1952

It provides for the following:

(i) Shelters for taking food and rest if 50 or more workers are employed;

(ii) First-aid boxes and first-aid rooms if more than 150 workers are employed;

(iii) A canteen, if 250 or more workers are employed;

(iv) A creche, if 50 or more women workers are employed;

(v) Pit-head baths equipped with showers, sanitary latrines;

(vi) Welfare Officer, if 500 or more workers are employed.

### The Motor Transport Workers Act, 1961

The motor transport undertakings are required to provide for their workers:

(i) First-aid facilities equipped with the prescribed contents, to be kept in every transport vehicle;

(ii) Medical facilities at the operating and halting centers;

(iii) Canteen, if employing 100 or more workers;

(iv) Clean, ventilated, well-lighted and comfortable rest-rooms at every place where motor transport workers are required to halt at night;

(v) Uniforms, raincoats to drivers, conductors and line checking staff for protection against rain and cold;

(vi) Prescribed amount of working allowance to the staff mentioned above.

### The Contract Labour (Regulation and Abolition) Act, 1970

This Act provides that the following amenities shall be made available by contractors for their employees:

(i) Canteen, if employing 100 or more workers;

(ii) Rest rooms or other suitable alternative accommodation where contract labour is required to halt at night in connection with the work of the establishment;

(iii) Washing facilities;

(iv) First-aid box equipped with the prescribed contents.

### Inter-State Migrant Workmen (Regulation and Employment and Conditions of Service) Act, 1979

Every contractor, employing inter-state migrant workmen, shall provide:

(i) Suitable conditions of work;

(ii) Suitable residential accommodation to workers during the period of their employment;

(iii) Medical facilities for workmen, free of charge;

(iv) Such protective clothing as may be prescribed.

### Role of the Welfare Officer

The model rules framed under the Factories Act, 1948, which was the pioneering legislation to provide for the appointment of welfare officers, had laid down a chart of duties for them. These duties are:

1. Supervision of

(a) safety, health and welfare programmes, such as housing, recreation, sanitation services as provided under law or otherwise.

(b) working of joint committees,

(c) grant of leave with wages as provided, and

(d) redress of workers' grievances.

2. Counselling workers in
   - (a) personal and family problems,
   - (b) adjusting to the work environment, and
   - (c) understanding rights and privileges.
3. Advising the management in
   - (a) formulating labour and welfare policies,
   - (b) apprenticeship-training programmes,
   - (c) meeting the statutory obligation to workers,
   - (d) developing fringe benefits, and
   - (e) workers' education and the use of communication media.
4. Liaising
   - (a) with workers to
     - (i) understand various limitations under which they work,
     - (ii) appreciate the need for harmonious indsutrial relations in the plant,
     - (iii) interpret company policies to workers, and
     - (iv) persuade them to come to a settlement in the case of a dispute.
   - (b) with the management to
     - (i) appreciate the workers' viewpoints in various matters in the plant,
     - (ii) intervene on behalf of the workers in matters under consideration of the management,
     - (iii) help different departmental heads to meet their obligations under the Act,
     - (iv) maintain harmonious industrial relations in the plant, and
     - (v) suggest measures for promoting the general well-being of workers.
   - (c) with workers and the management
     - (i) to maintain harmonious industrial relations in the plant,
     - (ii) for the prompt redress of grievances and the quick settlement of disputes, and
     - (iii) to improve the productive efficiency of the enterprise.

(d) with outside agencies, such as

(i) factory inspectors, medical officers and other inspectors for securing the proper enforcement of various Acts as applicable to the plant, and

(ii) other agencies in the community with a view to helping workers to make use of community services.

## Welfare Officer in Mines (Mines Rules 1955)

Welfare Officer: (1) For every mine wherein 500 or more persons are ordinarily employed, the owner, agent or manager shall appoint a suitably qualified person as Welfare Officer, and where the number of persons so employed in a mine exceeds 2,500 such Welfare Officer shall be assisted by one suitably qualified additional Welfare Officer for every additional 2,000 persons or part thereof employed.

(2) No person shall act as Welfare Officer of a mine unless he possesses:

(a) a university degree;

(b) a degree or diploma in social science (or social work) or labour welfare [recognised by the Government for the purpose of this rule] and preferably practical experience of handling labour problems in any industrial undertaking for at least three years; and

(c) a knowledge of the language of the district in which the mine is situated or the language understood by the majority of persons employed in the mine:

Provided that in case of a person already in service as a Welfare Officer in a mine, the above qualifications may, with the approval of the Chief Inspector, be relaxed.

[Notwithstanding anything contained in sub-rule (2) the Labour Officers included in the Central Pool under the provision of the Labour Officer (Central Pool) Recruitment and the Condition of Service Rules, 1951, shall be eligible for appointment as a Welfare Officer in a mine.]

(3) Where by reason of temporary absence, illness or any other similar cause, the Welfare Officer is unable to perform his duties the owner, agent or manager shall authorise in writing a person whom he considers competent, to act in his place:

Provided that no such authority shall have effect for a period in excess of 30 days except with the previous consent to the Chief Inspector or Inspector.

(4) A written notice of every appointment, authorisation, discharge, dismissal, resignation or termination of service of every Welfare Officer and of the date thereof shall be sent by owner, agent or manager to the Chief Inspector within seven days from the date of such appointment, authorisation, discharge, dismissal, resignation or termination of service.

(5) The post of Welfare Officer shall be advertised in a newspaper having a wide circulation in the State.

Duties of Welfare Officers: (1) The duties of Welfare Officers shall be:

(i) to establish contacts and hold consultations with a view to maintain harmonious relations between the management and persons employed in the mine;

(ii) to bring to the notice of the management the grievances of employees, individual as well as collective, with a view to securing their expeditious redressal;

(iii) to promote relations between management and employees which will ensure productive efficiency as well as amelioration in the working conditions and to help workers to adjust and adapt themselves to their working environments;

(iv) to assist in the formation of work and Joint Production Committees, Co-operative Societies and Safety, First Aid and Welfare Committees and to supervise their work;

(v) to help the management in regulating the grant of leave with wages and explain to the workers the provisions relating to leave with wages and other leave privileges and to guide the workers in the matter of submission of applications for grant of leave for regulating authorised absence;

(vi) to advise on welfare provisions, such as housing facilities, food stuffs, social and recreational facilities, sanitation, individual personal problem and education of children;

(vii) to supervise welfare activities statutory or otherwise, including education and training to employees;

(viii) to suggest measures which will tend to raise the standard of living of workers and in general promote their well-being; and

(ix) to perform any other duty connected with the welfare of the persons employed in the mine.

(2) Notwithstanding anything contained in sub-rule (1), no Welfare Officer shall deal with any disciplinary case against a person employed in a mine, or appear before a Conciliation Officer, Court or Tribunal on behalf of the management of a mine against a person or persons employed in the mine, except when he is required by the Conciliation Officer, Court or Tribunal to appear as an independent witness:

Provided that nothing in this sub-rule shall be deemed to prohibit a person employed in a mine from approaching the Welfare Officer in respect of a grievance arising out of any case of disciplinary action against him.

(3) Every Welfare Officer shall keep a record of his day-to-day work and shall at the end of every year forward to the Chief Inspector through the Manager of the mine concerned, a summary of the report of his work during the year.

Conditions of Service: (1) A Welfare Officer shall be given appropriate status corresponding to the status of the other executive heads of the mine.

(2) The conditions of service of a Welfare Officer shall be the same as of other members of the staff of corresponding status in the mine:

Provided that before the owner, agent or manager discharges or dismisses a Welfare Officer, who has satisfactorily completed a probationary period of six months, he shall consult the Chief Inspector or an Inspector authorised in this behalf by the Chief Inspector.

### Problems of stagnation and demotivation towards the welfare job in India

In order to study the basic issues surrounding the above problem, a Think Group was constituted to specifically seek answers to several important questions [Fr. John C. Prabhu S.J. (XLRI), H.S. Verma (Telco), S.N. Pandey (Tisco), P.T.K. Panicker (Tisco),

H.M. Jha (Tisco Mines), R. Luther (Tisco Collieries), N. Mishra (Tisco), Prof. C.G.K. Nair (XLRI), K.P. Verma (Tisco)]. While arriving at the answers to the questions, the Group considered the problems in a wider perspective taking the country as a whole, instead of restricting themselves to the region or the organizations in which they were working.

**Q.1.** What are the factors responsible for the decline of young people's interest in the welfare job?

(i) In every aspect of Personnel Management except welfare, a growth is discernible both in regard to the concept and the contents. But in respect of welfare there is a stagnation.

(ii) The young man of today wants to see the result of his efforts and that too quickly. On a welfare job he is told that the results are intangible and remote. The job therefore does not provide him with a challenge.

(iii) Personnel Officers engaged in other aspects of Personnel Management like Recruitment, Selection, Training, Wages and Salary Administration, Industrial Relations etc. are nearer to the Power Centres of the organizations and they therefore wield greater influence and authority than a welfare man who is very remote from the power centre. The young men wish to be near the power centre when they enter an organization.

(iv) In many organizations, industry or otherwise, personnel men are sometimes not required to possess a postgraduate qualification in Personnel Management or Labour Welfare. Ordinary graduates (and sometimes even unqualified men) are taken on these jobs.

(v) Welfare Officers with post graduate qualification mentioned above, are appointed by many organizations merely to satisfy the provisions of the law. They are paid less than personnel officers may be with the same qualifications or even less. Their status is also lower than that of Personnel Officers.

(vi) A welfare man has very little opportunity to do innovative or creative work. Organizations expect them to do only routine, traditional jobs like sports, canteens, creches, sanitation etc. mentioned in the law. Even in their management there is very little freedom for innovation or autonomy for action.

(vii) Opportunities of advancement for a qualified welfare man is limited whereas a personnel officer can go up to the top of the department.

(viii) The designation of Welfare Officer is out of date. Qualified men in this speciality should be given another designation so as to distinguish from others who are not professionally qualified.

**Q.2.** What are some of the socio-cultural variables contributing to the general demotivation towards the welfare job?

(i) There is a shift in emphasis from the paternalistic management to the professional. Every young man wishes to belong to a profession. They do not see any semblance of professionalism in welfare jobs as they are designed at present. The statutory provisions do not cater to this need.

(ii) Welfare is still being considered as the 'prerogative' of some old-timers who were once devoted social workers. These people do not like any change in the concept of welfare. They are also seen to wield some influence with industrial organizations, with the result that the welfare concept does not change.

(iii) The old concept of welfare was one of 'Missionary'. The urge of the newer generations is 'professionalism', but they still see the old concept persisting.

(iv) Inadequate status for a welfare man in the society today. People still say: "After all he is a man who should have a missionary zeal. He does not expect any recognition. So we need not worry about him."

(v) But if a person with the same background is a personnel officer he is looked at in a different manner, as belonging to a higher status by the society.

**Q.3.** What can industry do to motivate young people to take up welfare careers in industry?

(i) Industries should change their concept of welfare to one of professionalism rather than paternalism, and should appoint only people with professional qualifications with an aptitude for the job.

(ii) Industries should appreciate that the scope and contents of welfare are wider than mere sports and recreational activities or those mentioned in the law. Welfare connotes the development of the individual and the community within industry as well as outside in all their facets including leadership, discipline, self-help etc. Very few organizations have accepted and implemented this newer concept of welfare.

(iii) Inplant welfare has to be given a wider scope. It should not be restricted only to the provisions of the Factory Act or the Mines Act but should also extend to work environments on the job itself like work convenience, seating facilities, irritants caused by noise, glare, vibration etc.

(iv) The grade and salary structure of a professionaly qualified welfare man should be the same as a personnel man.

(v) Management of welfare to be re-oriented according to the latest management principles.

(vi) Job enrichment — An important method of motivation to be introduced in welfare jobs as well.

(vii) A qualified welfare man should be given an appropriate designation different from what it is today. In this connection, the changes that have come in the medical profession were cited. An E.N.T. specialist is called an 'Audio-Laringologist'; an Eye specialist is called Opthalmologist etc.

(viii) Managements should formulate their welfare policy as in the case of the other aspects of personnel policy.

**Q.4.** What can academic do in this respect?

(i) Students get an impression of a welfare job from the pattern prevailing in various organizations. In order to give them a correct idea, the 'success story' of some organizations who adopt welfare programmes of a nature different from the traditional ones should be told to the students by a practising welfare man belonging to such organizations. This will naturally have to be done by a professionally qualified person who could show the importance of welfare in the totality of Personnel Management.

(ii) The students will have to be shown the meaningful connection between their curriculum and the welfare jobs. But before doing so, the curricula in educational institutions should ensure that the welfare content is introduced in a greater degree instead of the scanty importance given to this aspect of personnel management in many of the curricula.

(iii) 'Management of welfare' should be a subject by itself, both its theory and practice.

(iv) The quality of intake in institutions teaching personnel management should be as rigid as for any other management subjects like finance, marketing etc.

(v) Greater practical orientation in welfare in the field should be imparted to the students. They should be able to see that challenges exist as much in welfare jobs as in any other jobs in personnel management. (Industries have a great role to play in this).

(vi) Students should be exposed in a greater measure to practising specialists in welfare and that too with those who are qualified professionally. Young students intending to be professional men do not readily accept a person who is not professionally qualified howsoever devoted and effective he may be in the eyes of the organization.

Where will industry's welfare man of tomorrow come from? Admittedly he must come from the institutions preparing young people for a professional career in the Personnel/HRM function. But how many of these young people are motivated by a welfare job? How many of them perceive the welfare job as a job as a powerful, challenging, serious proposition? How many of them see any long-term meaning and value in the pursuit of a welfare job in industry?

Answers to these disturbing questions, obtained on an impressionistic basis, point to an equally disturbing trend that not many young persons desire to have welfare as a career in Industry. This alarming trend does present a vital industrial problem of great concern to all welfare professionals.

# Workers' Participation in Management

# 20

The 'International Labour Organisation' in its Publication 'International Labour Review' rightly sums up the dilemma of the meaning of the concept of Workers' Participation in Management when it says that "the concept of Workers' Participation in Management means different things to different people; and most international discussions on the subject suffer from the fact that those who use the term are often thinking of one particular form of workers' participation in management. For the management, it is joint consultations prior to decision making. For labourers, it is just like co-decision or co-determination. For the administrators and experts, it is an association of labour with management without final authority or responsibility in decision making."

According to Prof. Keith Davis (Human Relations in Business): "It is a mental and emotional involvement of a person in a group situation, which encourages him to contribute to goals and share responsibilities in them."

J.P. Kesari and Gulzari Lal Nanda have stated thus:

"The concept of Workers' Participation in Management crystallises the concept of industrial democracy bringing in a new set of values both for the workers and the management, in which — 'Power' has been replaced by 'Persuasion', 'authoritarianism' by 'democracy' and 'compulsion' by 'co-operation'.

Mrityunjay Athreya (Organisational Determination of Participation) says, "At an atomic level, it could refer to the sense of involvement of an individual in his own life in its varied aspects. At the macro level, it could refer to the involvement of each individual citizen in the conduct of national life. At an intermediate stage, at the enterprise level, it could refer to the involvement of workers in the conduct of enterprise affairs."

Mhetras (1966) has suggested five levels of participation which range on a scale from minimum to maximum participation in decision making viz.

(i) Information Participation, (ii) Consultative Participation, (iii) Associative Participation, (iv) Administrative Participation and (v) Decision Participation.

Participation basically means 'Involvement'. There must be a concept of 'winning together'. The management should be able to convince the workers: "I need you; I need your talent. You are a valued member of this team and we must win together." In the Indian context, Workers' Participation in Management imbibes the concept of Industrial Democracy and Consequent 'involvement' of the workers in the management process by way of various degree of better communication and consultations between workers and management. Sometimes, the management gives scope to the workers to influence its decision-making and may share with them some of its managerial prerogatives.

Now, the extent or the kind of workers' involvement in the management process would depend on the industrial relations scenario and amongst other things — the philosophy or the outlook of the organisation towards their workforce.

### Forms of Workers' Participation in India

Workers Participation has been introduced in the following forms in Indian industries:

(i) The Works Committees: (Set up under the Industrial Disputes Act, 1947);

(ii) The Joint Management Councils: (Set up as the result of the Labour-Management Co-operation Seminar, 1958);

(iii) The Scheme of Worker Representatives on the Board of Management (under Management and Miscellaneous Scheme, 1970) on some public and private sector enterprises including industrial undertakings and nationalised banks;

(iv) Since July 1975, two-tier participation model, namely, the Shop Council, at the shop level and Joint Council at the enterprise level were introduced;

(v) In January, 1977, a new scheme of workers' participation in management in commercial and service organisations in the public sector undertakings was launched, with the setting up of the Unit Councils.

## Indian Experiments in Joint Consultation and Participative Management

The provision of Works Committee in the Industrial Disputes Act, 1947, with equal representation from employers and employees was intended to promote measures for securing and preserving good industrial relations through mutual discussion. In the absence of a strong trade union movement healthy collective bargaining relationship and any conviction on the part of employers, regarding the need for consulting labour, works committees did not prove an effective forum for solving problems and fostering good relations. Instead of a single works committee, in some organisations a number of joint committees for relations, production standard, wage fixation, safety, canteen, welfare etc. have been constituted for purposes of consultation. These joint consultative committees proved useful only in those organisations which had healthy practices of recognising representative trade unions and negotiating long-term settlements with them and mostly these committees emerged as the forum for solving day-to-day problems within the framework of the collective agreement concluded with the union and without trespassing into areas which come within the purview of collective bargaining. Later Joint Management Councils have been experimented in a few selected organisations which admittedly have ended in failure in the absence of commitment to the idea from both sides. Further, representatives have been taken as members of the Board of Directors of some public sector undertakings. Such sporadic experiments based on ideological or idealistic wishful thinking are not likely to succeed without developing a philosophical conviction and practical commitment among employers and employees to the idea. And this is possible only if long and laborious preparatory ground work is done by associating employees in day-to-day problems regarding work allocation and job performance at the shopfloor and consulting union representatives on production standards, performance rating, job rates, fringe benefits, welfare measures, disciplinary procedures, grievances etc. and negotiating agreements with the leadership of the union with regard to all terms and conditions of work. In other words, only after representative trade unions are recognised can collective bargaining take firm roots, only after collective bargaining has come to stay, can joint consultation be promoted and only after gaining experience with joint consultation can participative management be experimented with.

In the eagerness to bring about changes which are attractive from the ideological standpoint, if cart is put before the horse, the result can only be disappointing. If we are serious about participative management we should start with meaningful dialogue at the shopfloor level between supervisors and workers regarding work methods, work allocation, crew sizes, job description, time utilisation etc. The exchange of information and feelings at the shopfloor level should be informal and uninhibited by hierarchical structure and social gap. The atmosphere of formal negotiations with preplanned strategies and positions will be barriers to effective communication and it will not help to bridge the gap of understanding between management and employees. It is not enough if the employees' representatives are consulted; the employees should participate in decision-making in the area of work. To enable the supervisors to get employees involved in target-setting, decision-making, performance review etc. at the shop floor/office levels, the supervisory and junior management staff should be properly trained and oriented. Management has to acquire new skills and abilities to make workers participate effectively. All this needs thorough preparation of ground; it is not enough just to indulge in wishful thinking about sharing of power.

Let us examine whether the functions of the Works Committees, Joint Management Councils and Shop and Joint Councils, Fulfil the conditions necessary for becoming superordinate goals. The following questions needs to be answered in this regard:

Is it a compelling goal for management?

Is it a compelling goal for workers?

Are all workers involved in the goal attaining activity?

### A. Works Committees

1. Conditions of work such as ventilation, lighting, temperature, and sanitation including latrines and urinals.

2. Amenities such as drinking water, canteens, dining rooms, rest rooms, medical and health services.

3. Safety and accident preventation, occupational diseases and protective equipment.

4. Adjustment of festival and national holidays.

5. Administration of welfare and fine funds.

6. Educational and recreational activities.

7. Promotion of thrift and savings.

8. Implementation and review of decisions arrived at in meetings of Works Committees.

**B. Joint Management Councils**

9. Administration of the standing orders and their amendment.

10. Retrenchment.

11. Rationalization.

12. General economic situation of the concern, receive information, discuss and give suggestion.

13. The state of market, production and sales programme.

14. Organization and general running of the undertaking.

15. Circumstances affecting the general running of the undertaking.

16. Methods of manufacturing and work.

17. Annual balance sheet and profit and loss account and connected documents and explanations.

18. Long-term plan for expansions, redeployment, etc.

19. Administration of welfare measures, administrative responsibility.

20. Supervision of safety measures.

21. Operation of vocational training and apprenticeship schemes.

22. Preparation of schedules of working hours and of holidays.

23. Payments of rewards for valuable suggestions.

24. Assist management in achieving production targets.

25. Eliminate waste and assist in optimum use of man-power and machine capacity.

26. Eliminate pockets of inefficiency.

27. Help reduce absenteeism and increase discipline.

28. Help improve physical working conditions and safety measures.

29. Devise welfare measures.

30. To help in ensuring two-way communication between workers and management.

The above will need some explanation. The questions asked before have been drawn up on the basis of the following assumptions:

(i) Management, traditionally, is concerned with maximizing profits and any activity — that does not clearly promote that goal will not have compelling appeal for management.

(ii) Workers, traditionally, are interested in maximizing physiological, social and psychological satisfactions and any activity that does not promote any of these satisfactions will not have compelling appeal for them.*

(iii) Because there usually is greater homogeneity and cohesiveness in the ranks of management as regards goals, it is not important whether all members of management are involved in the goal — attaining activity.+

[*Participation in decision-making is widely believed to satisfy some of these needs. However, it is also Ishwar Dayal's contention that the Indian personality is dependence-prone, and would be more comfortable in a nurturing rather than in participant relationships at work.

+To adduce some evidence for this, Kelley found that the higher the position in the hierarchy (in an organization), the greater the attraction for other members of the group.]

An observation, made by an American scholar of the European industrial relations scene, is quite relevant to the current concern with the subject. "The issue, to what extent should workers participate in the management of the enterprise in which they are employed runs like a thread through twentieth-century European politics; it disappears only to appear again, for it has never really, been resolved satisfactorily. It is clearly part of socialism's unfinished business. And in this continuing discontent and failure to resolve the issue fully and finally, lies the dynamics for further change and experiment with various form of worker's management.

# Disciplinary Proceedings, Domestic Inquiries and Grievance Procedure

# 21

The Principles of Natural Justice are such principles which are considered vital to ensure justice and to give due protection to the employee whose conduct is under consideration. As a result of the disciplinary proceedings and domestic enquiry the punishment is likely to be inflicted upon an employee and therefore it is essential that justice is done in its true spirit.

The principles of natural justice are based on two maxims recognised in the English law. They are:

1. "Nemo debet esse judex in propria causa" — this means no one should be judged in his own case, and
2. "Adi ateram partem" — this means 'hear the other side'.

It will thus be seen that the whole concept of Natural Justice is towards "Fair Play", and the most important aspect of 'Fair Play' is that "Justice should not only be done but it should manifestly appear to be done."

However, the "Principles of Natural Justice" are not laws in themselves and therefore they cannot be elevated to the position of Fundamental Rights. Rather the aim of rules of Natural Justice is to secure justice or to put it negatively, to (Prevent) miscarriage of justice'.

It should be noted that standing orders are not applicable to all the industries and also that the standing orders cannot give an exhaustive list of misconducts. The primary meaning of the word 'misconduct' is bad management or mismanagement and malfeasance or culpable neglect or 'an act subversive of discipline'.

Now, the question arises as to what is 'subversive of discipline'? The word 'discipline' in the industrial or business concept is often narrowly interpreted. To many persons, the term means something rigid and negative almost tending to present a long list of 'don'ts' for the workers and lower levels of staff. In reality, however, discipline in the industry or business should mean performance of duties in an orderly manner, according to the prevailing work-rules and norms.

Absence of discipline in the workplace or 'indiscipline', is a serious problem in many organizations in India. It is not proper to think that workers alone are always to be blamed for indiscipline. Sometimes, management also has its share. Often the loose conduct, unpunctuality, or behaviour of the top or middle-level managers affect the 'culture' of the organization so much that it percolates to lower levels. Factionalism among the managers at times encourages them to favour one group or faction of the workers (or in the case of multiple unions, one of the unions) as against others in the expectation of narrow gains for their own particular managerial faction. There have been cases noted in Indian factories, that some executives indirectly encouraged the workers belonging to a favoured faction to behave rudely with the executives whom they disliked. Naturally this leads to indiscipline, which spreads like fire, and ultimately may not even spare those who helped it for their own narrow ends. Sometimes, indiscipline may occur because of the ignorance of the expected behaviour or rules of the workplace, which the management did not care to give due publicity to, or to explain to make them intelligible to the ordinary workers. In addition, indiscipline also may be due to bad labour-management relations, trade union's policy to excuse any wrong deeds of the workers, and the unfavourable image of the management, or their ineffectiveness or weakness. Indiscipline also may be encouraged by the lack of consistency of the management in dealing with the workers' lapses. At times, sheer frustration of the workers may lead to acts of indiscipline. If the workers feel that there is no remedy for their grievances to which the management would always be deaf, or if the conditions of work are so bad that the workers have lost their patience, often their frustration may find outlets in acts of indiscipline.

### Principles of Good Disciplinary Action

Although the management should always try to project their reasonable image and should be sympathetic to the difficulties, or unintentional minor lapses on the part of their workmen, serious acts of indiscipline should always be strictly and properly dealt with. But here good managers often face a dilemma. How should they enforce discipline, but at the same time would try to keep intact their image of reasonable managers? For this problem, Douglas McGregor has suggested his 'Red Hot-Stove Rule'. The rule is actually based on an analogy between violating rules of discipline and touching a hot stove which has turned red due to intense heat. Whenever, someone touches a hot stove, the impact on him is immediate, with warning, consistent and impersonal.

Everyone who touches a stove would experience an immediate burn, and the heat and the colour of the stove warns everybody about it. The burning would be consistent, because everyone who touches the hot stove would have it, irrespective of who touches it and when or why. Thus the lesson is impersonal; anyone who would dare to disregard the warning, would be punished by the burn. Similarly, good disciplinary system in a workplace should be based on a set of rules of conduct which themselves would also pronounce the penalties of violation for the purpose of warning. Penalties should be imposed consistently and impersonally, without any discrimination or favour for any person or position. The action should be taken immediately after the violation, and there should not be any unnecessary lag between the two. In general, the disciplinary action should not be vindictive or biased. It must be based on well-publicized policies and procedures and its main purpose should be to obtain compliance with the established rules of conduct.

### Legal Requirements of Disciplinary Action in Indian Industries

Under the Industrial Employment (Standing Orders) Act, 1946, every industrial establishment employing 100 or more workers (50 in West Bengal) has to define in its 'Standing Orders' the conditions of employment, including rules of discipline and penalties for their violation.

These standing orders are to be drafted by the employers and 5 copies of such drafts are to be submitted to the Certifying Officer under the Act. The latter is required to forward a copy thereof and a notice to the Trade Union for its comments and objections which must be submitted within 15 days from the receipt of the notice. After this, the Certifying Officer adjudicates over the reasonableness of the provisions of the draft standing order and the objections to them. The employers or the employees may appeal against the award of the C.O. The finally certified 'Standing Orders' (including the provisions for discipline) come into force on expiry of 30 days of certification, or on the expiry of 7 days on which the decision of the Appellate Authority is sent.

Under the Model Standing Orders appended to the Central rules framed under the Industrial Employment (Standing Orders) Act, certain acts of misconduct, (i.e., indiscipline) have been provided, and for these the worker or workers concerned may be suspended up to 4 days and later on dismissed according to the provisions of the certified standing orders. These acts include:

(1) Disobedience and wilful insubordination.

(2) Theft, fraud, dishonesty in connection with the employer's business or property.

(3) Wilful damage to or loss of employers' goods or property.

(4) Taking or giving bribes or any illegal gratification.

(5) Habitual absence without leave or absence without leave for more than 10 days.

(6) Habitual late attendance.

(7) Habitual breach of any law applicable to the establishment.

(8) Riotous or disorderly behaviour during working hours at the establishment, or any act subversive of discipline.

(9) Habitual negligence, or neglect of work.

(10) Frequent repetition of any act or omission for which fine may be imposed.

(11) Striking of work, or inciting others to strike in contravention of the provisions of any law.

Under the 'Model Standing Orders', the following procedure for punishment is provided. First, the concerned worker has to be given a 'charge-sheet' in writing, detailing the allegations of misconduct, specifying the particular provisions of the 'Standing Orders' under which the allegations are made. The worker has to be given the opportunity to explain his conduct or the circumstances alleged. Then an enquiry has to be held in which the worker concerned has to be given opportunity to adduce evidence in his favour, with a right to be accompanied or represented by fellow workmen, at the enquiry. In case of dismissal, the approval of the manager concerned or the employer is necessary and such an order has to be properly served on the workman. In case of suspension, the allegation has to be served on the worker in the form of a written charge-sheet, following the service of which the worker concerned may be suspended immediately. An enquiry has to follow the charge-sheet. If the order is confirmed, the worker would not be eligible to receive any remuneration for the period of suspension. If, however, the order is rescinded, he would be deemed to be on duty during the period of suspension and shall be entitled to his full pay for the period of suspension.

Apart from the provisions of the Standing Orders certified under the above mentioned Act, certain other legal conditions on discipline, misconduct and punishment have been evolved on the basis of various judgements passed by different judges in these respects. Firstly, discharge or dismissal without proper enquiry has been declared unlawful. Secondly, the order following the enquiry must conform to the principles of Natural Justice. However, a Labour Court, a Tribunal, or National Tribunal, adjudicating on the discharge or dismissal being the punishment inflicted by the management on the basis of the enquiry, can set it aside, if the order of discharge or dismissal is unjustified, or based on basic errors of facts, or perverse findings. It can direct the management to reinstate the workman or can reduce the punishment, or give any other relief to him that it thinks fit.

## Domestic Enquiries

The enquiry which is conducted about the allegations of misconduct of a worker by the persons authorized to do so by its management, is usually described as 'domestic enquiry'. Under the domestic enquiry, no person who is directly interested in the outcome of the enquiry is appointed as an Enquiry Officer for that purpose. He must be disinterested either in the complainant, or the charge-sheeted workman, or in the subject-matter of the enquiry. It is preferable that he should not be the executive who has issued the charge-sheet himself or would ultimately take the disciplinary action, if warranted by the enquiry. For holding domestic enquiries, the Enquiry Officer should ensure that certain conditions are fulfilled. It is essential that sufficient notice is given to the workman for the enquiry that he may have enough time to prepare his defence and to make ready all documents which he desires to produce as evidence. The enquiry is to be held in the presence of the accused. If, however, the notice is properly served but the accused workman does not turn up before the enquiry

Officer without any notice or proper reason, it may be held ex-parte. The findings of the Enquiry Officer are to be based on the facts of the case and the documents produced. He should send his report to the management for proper action. In case of any punishment, the order has to be communicated to the worker concerned as quickly as possible.

## Grievance Procedure

It has been noted above that in many cases, acts of indiscipline may result from the workers' accumulated grievances which go unattended. A suitable 'Grievance Procedure', working as a built-in mechanism, may help reduce such indiscipline to a great extent.

A good 'Grievance Procedure' which is expected to show results usually possesses the following characteristics. First, it should be mutually acceptable to the management and the Union, and should not be unilaterally imposed. Secondly, it should possess several well-defined steps for handling grievances, each step on its failure being followed by another step for higher-level handling. The number of steps naturally would depend on the size of the organization and the composition of the workforce. It is desirable that the Procedure should be simple and not legalistic. It should also provide for reference of the grievances to voluntary arbitration, if no mutually acceptable settlement is possible at the highest level. For its success, it is further essential that at each stage the grievance procedure should be time-bound. In other words, excessive or unreasonable delay in considering the grievance at any stage should be avoided. The National Commission on Labour in its Report stated that Grievance Procedure should be simple and have provision for at least one appeal. The procedure should ensure that it gives a sense of (i) satisfaction to the individual workers, (ii) reasonable exercise of authority to the manager, and (iii) participation of unions. The Commission prefers that a grievance procedure should normally provide for three steps:

(a) Approach to the immediate superior;

(b) Appeal to the departmental head or manager; and

(c) Appeal to the bipartite grievance committee representing management and the recognized Union.

In some organizations, the Grievance Procedure contains more steps, mainly to avoid burdening the top management and the Union leadership with grievances which could be settled at intermediate steps. The steps in one such 'Grievance Procedure' mechanism are given below:

| Step | Representing the employee/union | Representing management |
|---|---|---|
| I. | Employee and /or Union representative in the department | Foreman |
| II. | Union secretary or the shop steward | General Foreman or Head of the Department |
| III. | Grievance Committee of the union or a team of union representatives including the union secretary | Chief Personnel Manager or Director of Personnel, or Director of Labour Relations |
| IV. | A team of union representatives including the union secretary and the President | Plant Manager or General Manager |

Whatever may be the 'Grievance Procedure', it is advisable that it should be sanctioned by a collective agreement between the management and the union. Where there is no such agreement, the procedure should be detailed in the 'Standing Orders' of the organization, certified under the provisions of the Industrial Employment (Standing Orders) Act, 1946. It should be clearly mentioned in the Grievance Procedure that if no settlement is possible at the highest level of the negotiations between the union and the management, the matter may be referred to an arbitrator, mutually acceptable to both side.

### Grievance Settlement Authority

In the year 1982, Chapter IIB was inserted in the 'Industrial Disputes Act', providing the setting up of Grievance Settlement Authorities for reference of certain industrial disputes. Under this provision, every industry employing fifty or more workmen has to set up a grievance settling authority, within the establishment, to settle disputes of individual workmen employed in that establishment. The trade unions or the workmen are required to refer their grievances to this authority, which will process the disputes in the prescribed manner. No reference to the courts or tribunals can be made unless the dispute is first referred to this authority.

### Case Study on 'Grievance Filters'

Let us consider an imaginary situation. Mr. "X" is a union official who has had some trouble with the medical officer of his company in connection with his child's health. The child suffered a lot and died of amnesia. This was considered by "X" as a professional incompetence on the part of the doctor. So "X" went and reported to his departmental head about this, but the latter had no control over the Medical Officer and could take no direct action against him. So, he sent a memo to the superintendent's office with regard to the matter. Unfortunately, the memo got misplaced. Since no action was taken on the memo, "X" took it as an insult. So he went straight and reported to the General Manager that he was discriminated against by the management because of the inefficient administration. He also accused the superintendent of being partial and behaving like a capitalist agent. But the General Manager was a busy person and could not personally look into the matter. So, he directed "X" to deliver his complaint to the Chief Medical Officer. When "X" went to the Chief Medical Officer the latter was busy conducting a crucial surgery and thus "X" could not meet him. Next day, when he went to him again he had left headquarters to attend a medical conference elsewhere. So "X" had to wait for three days before the Chief Medical Officer returned. This left the complainant boiling with anger yet unable to solve the problem. Later when he met the Chief Medical Officer he blamed him and his colleagues with regard to their conduct and efficiency. As it is clear before us, the grievance here had already been filtered twice. This indisciplined behaviour of "X" upset the Chief Medical Officer as arguments took heated turn. He could not possibly allow the serene hospital atmosphere to be disrupted by such noise as was created because of the arguments. So he had no other way out but to ask "X" to get out of the hospital. This caused further tension and the union did not like one of his officials to get such an 'ill-treatment' from the management. But it remained unrevealed before the mass that "X"'s child was suffering from a more or less incurable disease and fell victim to it.

The enraged "X" felt as if a second fatal blow was being dealt to him in addition to his child's death when he was given a charge sheet, for misbehaving with the Chief Medical Officer in the hospital. He also felt that the company was not paying the workers well for which they could not afford treatment for themselves or their family members in other hospitals. Under the circumstances, it was quite easy for him to convince his union colleagues on this issue and make them share his own feelings. Thus, the union came up with the consensus that management of the company was earning lump sum profits by exploiting the labour and paying them low wages.

Here we find that the original grievance has undergone further filters and has become much more effectively shaded by almost non-existent issues. Coming back to our example, the union easily convinced the workers, about its stand and got their immediate support. So they took a decision to go on strike demanding immediate wage risk and also requesting the Government to nationalise the company in order to counter the so-called "inefficient management" of the company.

This shows how a grievance can take a severe turn and affect the entire organization. It is, therefore, necessary to reach the grievance before filters set in.

# Industrial Disputes Act, 1947

# 22

The Industrial Disputes Act, 1947, is a legal regulation of conflict resolution.

This Act was brought in to make provisions for the investigation and settlement of industrial disputes and for certain other purposes. It applies to the whole of India and to all the industrial establishments.

Some of the important definitions under this enactment are discussed so that the reader will get a fair understanding of the coverage of this law, its applicability and scope.

### Industry

As per the law the word industry means any business, trade, undertaking, manufacturing or calling of employers and includes any calling service, employment, handicraft or industrial occupation or a vocation of workmen.

This definition of industry is broad. However, it does not cover all employer-employee relations. To understand this one needs to keep the following factors in mind:

(a) The activity carried out must be systematic and organized.

(b) There must be organized basic co-operation between employer and employees.

(c) The objective should be production and or distribution of goods and services to satisfy the human wants or desires.

Judgment given in the case of Bangalore Water Supply and Sewerage Board vs. A. Rajappa has played an important role in clarifying the definition given in the Act and also in moulding the nature of industry for future guidance. It is held in this case (1978, II, LLJ 73 (SC) that the application of the Act is so comprehensive that it covers every kind of organized activity undertaken with the co-operation of the employees for the production and for distribution of goods and services calculated to satisfy human wants and wishes, irrespective of who undertakes it, with what motive it is undertaken, or what is the number of workmen with the help of whom it is undertaken.

In the year 1982, the Act was amended to substitute the definition of "Industry". However, the revised definition is not yet enforced, hence the position referred above still continues.

### Appropriate Government

This is a Central enactment. However, the Act provides for two separate machineries for dispute redressals to be constituted by, namely the State Government in respect of its own State and the Central Government in respect of certain undertakings irrespective of their locations.

Central Government is the appropriate Government in respect of the industries specified in Section 2(a) (i), and the State Government is the appropriate Government in respect of the industries specified in Section 2 (a) (ii).

### Industrial Dispute

An industrial dispute is dispute or difference between an employer and his workmen which is connected with the employment or non-employment, or the terms of employment, or the conditions of labour of any person.

An industrial dispute comes into existence as and when a demand is made by either an employer or the workmen on any of the matters illustrated above and the other party refuses to concede the demand. The demand need not necessarily be made in writing and also need not necessarily be made directly on the employer.

Normally an individual dispute, meaning a dispute related to an individual workman cannot be treated as an industrial dispute. However, such a dispute can be treated as an industrial dispute, if it is supported by a Union or a group of workmen, or in case of an individual dispute related to dismissal, discharge, retrenchment or termination of employment of the workman.

It may be noted that a workman who is dismissed, discharged or retrenched or where service is otherwise terminated, will continue to be covered under this Act.

### Workman

A workman means and includes any person who is employed in an industry for doing any manual, unskilled, skilled, technical, operational, clerical or supervisory work for hire or reward. This includes any of those persons who are dismissed, discharged or retrenched in connection with, or as a consequence of that dispute, or where dismissal, discharge or retrenchment has led to that dispute. This definition does not include:

1. Army, Air Force or Defence Personnel,
2. Police and Prison Personnel,
3. Those who are employed in supervisory capacity and draw wages in excess of Rs. 1600/- p.m., or even those who exercise powers vested in them and have functions mainly of managerial nature.

This Act specifically includes apprentices under the ambit of the definition.

While deciding whether a person is a workman or not, one will have to specifically examine the nature of work carried out by him. The designation of such a person has no relevance whatsoever.

### Notice of Change

In order that disputes do not arise or erupt due to sudden decisions of the employer wherein the employees are taken by surprise, the Act has made certain provisions. In the fourth schedule of the Act, certain conditions of service are specified, for which a notice of change has to be given. These service conditions are:

1. Wages, including the period and mode of payment.
2. Contribution paid, or payable, by the employer to any provident fund, or pension fund, or for the benefit of the workmen under any law for the time being in force;
3. Compensatory and other allowances;
4. Hours of work and rest intervals;
5. Leave with wages and holidays;
6. Starting, alteration or discontinuance of shift working otherwise than in accordance with standing orders;
7. Classification by grades;

8. Withdrawal of any customary concession or privilege, or change in usage;
9. Introduction of new rules of discipline, or alteration of existing rules, except in so far as they are provided in standing orders;
10. Rationalisation, standardisation or improvement of plant or technique which is likely to lead to retrenchment of workmen;
11. Any increase or reduction (other than casual) in the number of persons employed or to be employed in any occupation or process or department or shift, not occasioned by circumstances over which the employer has no control.

The notice is to be given in prescribed manner and no change should be affected within 21 days of giving such a notice. However, no notice of change is required for change in conditions following as a result of a settlement of award.

## Authorities under the Act

Under this Act some authorities are constituted for the prevention, investigation and settlement of industrial disputes. These are:

1. **Works Committee.** This is primarily constituted for prevention of industrial disputes.
2. **Court of Inquiry.** This has an objective of investigation of industrial disputes.
3. **Conciliation Officer and Board of Conciliation.** These are constituted for mediating between the disputing parties and promoting the settlements in the disputes.
4. **Labour Courts, Industrial Tribunals and National Tribunals.** These are constituted for settlement of disputes through the process of adjudication.

The Works Committee is constituted by the employer as per the guidelines specified by the law while other authorities are appointed by the appropriate Governments. Central Government is an appropriate Government in respect of industries specified by the law while respective State Governments are appropriate in relation to other industries. Some of the industries under the purview of Central Government machinery are: Air India, Indian Airlines, LIC, The Unit Trust of India, certain banking and insurance companies etc.

### Works Committee

In any industrial establishment which employs one hundred or more workmen, the appropriate Government may by either a general order or a specific order require the employer of such an industry to constitute a Works Committee in the concerned industry. The manner of constituting such a Works Committee will be prescribed by the appropriate Government.

The Works Committee has a duty to promote measures for securing and preserving amity and good relations between the employer and workmen and to that end, to comment upon the matters of their common interest or concern and endeavour to sort out any material difference of opinion in respect of such matters.

### Conciliation

A conciliation officer is an authority prescribed under the Act, for holding conciliation proceedings and promoting the settlement of disputes. If an occasion arises, the appropriate Government may appoint a Board of Conciliation for promoting and settling an industrial dispute.

The conciliation officer or the Board of Conciliation as the case may be, is charged with a duty to mediate in and promote the settlement of industrial disputes.

Whenever an industrial dispute arises or even is apprehended in a public utility service and when a notice of strike is served under section 22 in respect thereof, it becomes incumbent on a conciliation officer to hold conciliation proceedings in respect of that dispute. However, in other cases, it is not incumbent on him to do so. Depending on the merits of the case he may decide to admit a dispute in conciliation. A conciliation officer has no power to decide or adjudicate on a dispute. He is entrusted only with a responsibility to mediate and induce parties to come to a fair and amicable settlement, if he succeeds and brings about a settlement, and he has to make a report of the settlement to the Government. In case a Conciliation Officer or a Board of Conciliation as the case may be, fails to settle the dispute between the parties under the conciliation, a failure report is submitted to the Government. If the Government at its sole discretion decides, this dispute may be referred to the Labour Court, the tribunal or the national tribunal as the case may be for adjudication. Such a decision of reference is an administrative act and ordinarily cannot be challenged in court of law. However, it may be noted that the Government is bound to refer the dispute for adjudication in any of the following circumstances:

(a) If the dispute relates to a public utility service and the notice of strike is given in respect thereof.

(b) If parties to the dispute jointly or severally apply to the Government for making a reference for adjudication.

A tribunal or court has to confine its adjudication to only the points which are specified in the order of reference and the same has no jurisdiction to decide any matter which is not referred to it.

### Arbitration

This Act also provides for another machinery to settle the disputes. Disputes which either exist or are apprehended can be referred to voluntary arbitration if the employer and workmen agree for such reference. Any time before a dispute is referred to the labour court, tribunal or a national tribunal by a written agreement between the parties the dispute can be referred to the arbitration.

When a dispute is referred in the above manner, the Government on being satisfied that the majority of the parties are making a reference, shall publish a notification in the prescribed manner. On the issuance of such notification, the employers and the workmen who are not party to the arbitration are given an opportunity to present their case before the arbitrator. The arbitrator has to hear points of view of both the parties and then pass an award, which is submitted to the Government. Award of an arbitrator is binding on all the parties concerned.

The Arbitration Act does not apply to arbitration under this Act.

### Adjudication

The disputes which cannot be settled during either arbitration or conciliation may be referred for adjudication before any of the following judicial authorities constituted under the Act:

(a) Labour Courts

(b) Tribunals

(c) National Tribunals

***Labour Courts*:** These are the courts constituted by the appropriate Government by notification in the Official Gazette, for the adjudication of industrial disputes. The matters that could be referred to such courts are specified in the second schedule of the Act, which reads as follows:

1. The propriety or legality of an order passed by an employer under the standing orders;
2. The application and interpretation of standing orders;
3. Discharge or dismissal of workmen including reinstatement of or grant of relief to, workmen wrongfully dismissed;
4. Withdrawal of any customary concession or privilege;
5. Illegality or otherwise of a strike or lock-out; and
6. All matters other than those specified in the third schedule.

***Tribunals***: Tribunals or industrial tribunals are constituted by the appropriate Government by notification in the Official Gazette, for the adjudication of industrial disputes. The matters that could be referred for adjudication to such tribunals are specified in the third schedule of the Act. The matters which are in the second schedule could also be referred to the tribunals. These matters are the following:

1. Wages, including the period and mode of payment;
2. Compensatory and other allowances;
3. Hours of work and rest intervals;
4. Leave with wages and holidays;
5. Bonus, profit sharing, provident fund and gratuity;
6. Shift working otherwise than in accordance with standing orders;
7. Classification by grades;
8. Rules of discipline;
9. Rationalisation;
10. Retrenchment of workmen and closure of establishment; and
11. Any other matter that may be prescribed.

***National Tribunals***: The National Tribunals are constituted by the Central Government by notification in the Official Gazette. These tribunals are constituted for the adjudication of the disputes which in the opinion of the Central Government involve question of national importance or one of such a nature that industrial establishments situated in more than one state are likely to be interested in or affected by such disputes.

The Labour Courts, industrial tribunals and national tribunals are not bound by strict procedures in the proceedings before them. The provisions of the Evidence Act, in their strict sense are not applicable in the proceedings before them. They have discretion to follow any procedure they may think fit subject to the rules made under the Act.

Such courts and the tribunals have now received express powers to set aside any order of discharge or dismissal and direct reinstatement of the discharged or dismissed workmen if they are satisfied that the order of discharge or dismissal was not justified. While deciding the cases of disputes related to dismissal or discharge if the courts or tribunals are of the opinion that the punishment was disproportionate to the gravity of misconduct, then the courts/tribunals are empowered to set aside the orders of dismissal or discharge and substitute the same with lesser punishment. In case a labour court or tribunal by its award directs the reinstatement of any workmen, and the employer makes an appeal in a High Court or Supreme Court the employer is liable to pay such workman during the pendency of such proceedings full wages last drawn by him, inclusive of any maintenance allowance admissible to him under any rule, till such time the higher court does not decide the case.

### Settlements and Awards

1. A settlement could be arrived at, between employer and the workmen otherwise than in the course of conciliation proceedings. Such bipartite settlements have a binding character only on the parties to the agreement.

2. As against the above, a settlement signed and arrived at, during the conciliation proceedings which is tripartite in nature award of an arbitrator, and the awards passed by the labour court, tribunal or national tribunal are enforceable and binding on:

(i) All the parties to the dispute;

(ii) All parties summoned to appear in the proceedings. If the party referred to is an employer, his heirs, successors or assign or in respect of that establishment. If the party referred to is composed of workmen, all the persons employed in the establishment to which the dispute relates, on the date of dispute and also to all persons who subsequently become employees of that establishment.

3. A settlement comes into operation on the date agreed upon by the parties. If no date is agreed upon, the date on which the memorandum of settlement is signed by the parties will be the date of coming into the operation of the settlement.

4. A settlement is binding on the parties to the agreement for the period agreed upon and if no period is agreed upon, then the settlement has a binding effect for six months from the date of signing of the memorandum of settlement by the parties to the dispute and continues to be binding on the parties after the expiry of period aforesaid until two months from the date on which a notice in writing of an intention to terminate the settlement is given by one of the parties to the other party or parties.

5. An award remains in operation for a period of one year from the date it becomes enforceable. It becomes enforceable after thirty days from the date of its publication by the government or the date specified in the same.

6. After a settlement or an award is terminated, the parties are at liberty to raise fresh dispute. However, the settlement or award would continue to govern the terms and conditions of employment of the concerned workmen so long as it is not substituted by a fresh settlement or an award.

### Representation of Parties

1. Any party to a dispute is protected from appointing a lawyer to represent it in any conciliation proceedings unless the other party gives consent and the concerned court or tribunal as the case may be, gives a specific permission. Once a party gives consent for appearance of a legal practitioner, it cannot be subsequently withdrawn. Similarly, once a tribunal or court grants permission for appearance of a legal practitioner, it cannot be subsequently withdrawn.

2. A workman who is party to the dispute can appoint any one of the following, to appear on his behalf before or during any of the proceedings under the Act:

(a) If he is a member of a trade union then by any member of the executive or other office bearer of the union.

(b) If the union is in affiliation to a federation of a trade union, then by any member of the executive or other office bearer of such union.

(c) If he is not a member of any trade union by any member of the executive or other office bearer of any trade union connected with or by any other workman employed in the industry in which he is employed.

3. An employer who is a party to a dispute can be represented by any of the following, during the proceedings under this Act:

(a) If he is member of an association of employers, by any officer of such an association.

(b) If such an association is associated to a federation of associations of employers, by an officer of such federation.

(c) If he is not a member of any association of employers, by an officer of any association of employers connected with or by any other employer engaged in the industry in which he is engaged.

## Appeal

An award passed by a court or a tribunal under this Act, cannot be questioned by any court in any manner whatsoever and is deemed to be final. No suit can be filed for declaring any award void. However, a writ petition in a High Court can be filed, or an appeal by special leave to the Supreme Court against an award could also be filed.

## Strikes and Lockouts

Under this Act, no workman employed in a public utility service can go on strike and no employer in a public utility service shall lockout any of his workmen:

1. Without giving six weeks' notice before the strike or lockout as the case may be;
2. Within fourteen days of giving such a notice;
3. Before expiry of the date of strike, or lockout as the case may be, specified in such notice;
4. During the pendency of any conciliation proceedings and seven days after conclusion of such proceedings.

In other establishments no workmen employed in any industrial establishment shall go on strike, or no employer of any industrial establishment shall declare a lockout:

1. During the pendency of conciliation proceedings before a conciliation officer, or a Board of Conciliation and seven days after the conclusion of the proceedings.
2. During pendency of proceedings before a court or tribunal under the Act and two months after the conclusion of such proceedings. The same rule applies in case of arbitration proceedings.
3. When a settlement or award is in force during the period of service for any matter covered in the same contravention of above provisions will make a strike or lockout illegal, if a strike or lockout has already commenced in pursuance of an industrial dispute and is in existence at the time of reference of the dispute to the conciliation, arbitration, court, or a tribunal, the continuance of such a strike or lockout will not be deemed to be illegal if otherwise it is legal. However, the government may by an order prohibit the continuance of such a strike or lockout.

A strike or a lockout does not bring any break in the continuity of service as the contract of employment does not break by such an Act.

It is held in the case Crompton Greaves Ltd. vs. Workmen (1978, II, LLJ 80 SC) that the workmen who proceed on a strike can claim wages for the period of strike if the strike is legal, justified and peaceful. A strike is legal if it is not in breach of any law. It is justified if the reasons for it are not perverse. It is peaceful if no force or violence or sabotage is resorted to. If a lockout is declared as illegal, the workmen can claim wages for the period of lockout.

### Lay-Off

As and when an employer is unable to give work to an employee due to any of the following circumstances, the employer can lay-off the workmen from the duties:

(a) On account of shortage of coal, power, or raw materials; or

(b) Due to accumulation of stocks; or

(c) Due to break-down of machinery; or

(d) Due to natural calamity.

In event of a lay-off, the workmen who are laid-off are entitled to receive a lay-off compensation at the rate of 50% of the basic wages and dearness allowance. It may be noted that, this provision is not applicable to the establishments employing less than 50 workmen. It may also be noted that, the laid-off workmen are not entitled to any compensation under certain circumstances as mentioned in Section 25C and 25E of the Act.

It is held that during the lay-off, the contract of service is suspended, hence the lay-off compensation is not treated as wages.

### Retrenchment

Retrenchment is defined as termination by the employer of the services of a workman for any reasons whatsoever, but does not include the following:

(a) Voluntary retirement by the workmen.

(b) Termination due to punishment inflicted by way of a disciplinary action.

(c) Retirement of the workman on reaching the age of superannuation if the same is expressly specified in the contract of employment.

(d) Termination as a result of non-renewal of contract, i.e., due to afflux of the time.

(e) Termination due to continuous ill-health of a workman. If an employer desires to retrench a workman he needs to pay him the following:

   (a) Either gives one month's notice showing reasons for retrenchment or pay salary in lieu of the same,

   (b) At the time of retrenchment compensation at the rate of 15 days average pay for every year of service.

The employer in addition, requires giving to the Government a notice in the prescribed manner. In case of retrenchment, the principle of last come first go has to be followed and in event of employment opportunities, the retrenched workman should be re-employed in the organisation.

### Closures

Closure is defined as a permanent closing down of a place of employment or even a part thereof.

In case of closure and even in case of change in proprietorship of the concern if services of the workman are interrupted, a closure compensation at the rate of retrenchment compensation is payable to the workman. The employer is required to give a notice of at least sixty days before the date of intended closure to the Government and to the employees in a prescribed manner giving reasons for the closure. This provision is not applicable to the establishments employing less than fifty persons, or to an undertaking set up for construction work or project.

### Special Provisions for Lay-Off, Retrenchment and Closure

In an undertaking wherein more than a hundred persons are employed, if any of the action like lay-off, retrenchment and closure are intended, prior permission of the Government appropriate to that establishment is essential. Such permission may be sought by making an application in the prescribed format sixty days prior to intended action. The employer can take the intended action if permission is granted or no communication is received by him from the Government within the sixty days of submission of application.

The appropriate Government can, either on its own or on the application made by the employer, or any workman, review its order or refer the matter to a tribunal for the adjudication.

For retrenching, the employer is required to give to the workmen three months' notice, or pay in lieu of the same.

### Actions Restricted Against Workmen During Pendency of Proceedings

As and when a dispute is pending, certain restrictions are imposed on the employer's right to dismiss the workmen. Such restrictions are as follows:

1. If an employer needs to dismiss or discharge a workman for a misconduct during the pendency of any conciliation, arbitration or adjudication proceedings in respect of a dispute, in which the concerned workman is involved and if the misconduct is connected with the dispute, the employer has to make an application before the authority before which the proceeding is pending and obtain prior written permission before the intended action. In absence of such a permission, the management's action will be termed as invalid.

2. If an employer desires to discharge or dismiss a workman for any misconduct during the pendency of a dispute in either conciliation or adjudication and if the workman is concerned with such a dispute, but the misconduct is not connected with the same, the employer is expected to pay one month's salary to such a workman prior to dismissal or discharge and also obtain prior permission from the authority before whom the dispute is pending. If such permission is not obtained the order of the employer will be treated as invalid.
3. In case of a protected workman, if the employer desires to terminate his services either for a misconduct or otherwise or to dismiss or discharge a protected workman during the pendency of any conciliation, arbitration or adjudication proceedings in respect of a dispute in which the workman is involved, the employer is required to take prior permission by applying before the authority before whom the dispute is pending.

If a workman is discharged or dismissed in contravention of any of the above three, the workman may file a complaint to the authority before whom the dispute is/was pending. On receipt of such a complaint the concerned authority will decide not only on the contravention but also on the merits of the complaint and grant appropriate relief.

If the above authority is a court or a tribunal, the same can adjudicate the matter, and if it is before the conciliation officer, he has to mediate in the matter and try to promote a settlement.

### Restrictions on Alteration of Service Conditions

The employer's freedom to alter the service conditions of a workman who is concerned with a dispute, is restricted as follows when the dispute is pending:

1. If the dispute is pending before any of the authorities under the Act and if the subject matter of alteration is connected with the dispute, the employer must obtain permission of the concerned authority prior to such alteration. If subject matter is not connected with the dispute such permission is not required.
2. In case of protected workmen, during pendency of any dispute before an authority in which the workman is

concerned, the employer must obtain prior permission before alteration of any service condition irrespective of the subject matter.

If any alterations are affected in contravention of the above, the court/tribunal before whom the dispute is pending can adjudicate on receipt of a complaint as if the dispute was referred to them.

### Unfair Labour Practices

In 1982, by way an amendment the Central Government added a new Chapter V-C to the Act. By way of this amendment a fifth schedule is added to the Act, which gives a list of unfair labour practices on part of both workmen and the employer and prohibits both of them to indulge in the same.

The unfair labour practices identified are as follows:

I. On the part of employers and trade unions of employers

1. To interfere with, restrain from, or coerce, workmen in the exercise of their right to organise, form, join or assist a trade union or to engage in concerted activities for the purpose of collective bargaining or other mutual aid or protection, that is to say:
   (a) threatening workmen with discharge or dismissal, if they join a trade union,
   (b) threatening a lock-out or closure, if a trade union is organized,
   (c) granting wage increase to workmen at crucial periods of trade union organisation, with a view to undermining the efforts of the trade union organisation.
2. To dominate, interfere with or contribute support, financially or otherwise to any trade union that is to say:
   (a) an employer taking an active interest in organising a trade union of his workmen; and
   (b) an employer showing partiality or granting favour to one of several trade unions attempting to organise his workmen or to its members, where such a trade union is not a recognised trade union.
3. To establish employer sponsored trade unions of workmen.

4. To encourage or discourage membership in any trade union by discriminating against any workman, that is to say:
   (a) discharging or punishing a workman, because he urged other workmen to join or organise a trade union.
   (b) discharging or dismissing a workman for taking part in any strike (not being a strike which is deemed to be an illegal strike under this Act).
   (c) changing seniority rating of workmen because of trade union activities.
   (d) refusing to promote workmen to higher posts on account of their trade union activities.
   (e) giving unmerited promotions to certain workmen with a view to creating discord amongst other workmen, or to undermine the strength of their trade union.
   (f) discharging office-bearers or active members of the trade union on account of their trade union activities.
5. To discharge or dismiss workmen
   (a) by way of victimisation.
   (b) not in good faith, but in the colourable exercise of the employer's rights.
   (c) by falsely implicating a workman in criminal case on false evidence or on concocted evidence.
   (d) for patently false reasons.
   (e) on untrue or trumped up allegations of absence without leave.
   (f) in utter disregard of the principles of natural justice in the conduct of domestic enquiry or with undue haste.
   (g) for misconduct of a minor or technical character, without having any regard to the nature of the particular misconduct or the past record or service of the workman, thereby leading to a disproportionate punishment.
6. To abolish the work of a regular nature being done by workmen, and to give such work to contractors as a measure of breaking a strike.
7. To transfer a workman malafide from one place to another, under the guise of following management policy.

8. To insist upon individual workman, who are on a legal strike to sign a good conduct bond as a precondition to allowing them to resume work.
9. To show favouritism or partiality to one 'set' of workers regardless of merit.
10. To employ workmen as "badlis", casuals or temporary workmen and to continue them as such for years, with object of depriving them of the status and privileges of permanent workmen.
11. To discharge or discriminate against any workman for filing charges or testifying against an employer in any enquiry or proceeding relating to any industrial dispute.
12. To recruit workmen during a strike which is not an illegal strike.
13. Failure to implement award, settlement or agreement.
14. To indulge in acts of force or violence.
15. To refuse to bargain collectively in good faith with the recognised trade unions.
16. Proposing or continuing a lock-out deemed to be illegal under this Act.

II. On the part of workmen and trade unions of workmen:

1. To advise or actively support or instigate any strike deemed to be illegal under this Act.
2. To coerce workmen in the exercise of their right to self organisation or to join a trade union or refrain from joining any trade union, that is to say:
   (a) for a trade union or its members to picketing in such a manner that non-striking workmen are physically debarred from entering the work places;
   (b) to indulge in acts of force or violence or to hold out threats of intimidation in connection with a strike against non-striking workmen or against managerial staff.
3. For a recognised union to refuse to bargain collectively in good faith with the employer.
4. To indulge in coercive activities against certification of a bargaining representative.

5. To stage, encourage or instigate such forms of coercive actions as wilful "go-slow", squatting on the work premises after working hours or "gherao" of any of the members of the managerial or other staff.
6. To stage demonstrations at the residences of the employers or the managerial staff members.
7. To incite or indulge in wilful damage to the employer's property connected with the industry.
8. To indulge in acts of force or violence or to hold out threats of intimidation against any workman with a view to prevent him from attending work.

If a person commits any of the unfair labour practices, he can be punished with an imprisonment up to 6 months or with a fine up to Rs. 1000 or with both.

### Offences and Penalties

The Act provides for various offences and penalties. Some of them are given below:

1. Imprisonment up to a period of one month, or a fine up to Rs. 50 or both in event of:
   (a) commencement or continuation or abetting an illegal strike.
   (b) commencing, continuing or abetting an illegal lockout.
2. Imprisonment up to a period of six months or a fine up to Rs. 1000 or both, in event of:
   (a) Instigating or inciting or knowingly spending money for illegal strike or lockout.
   (b) Breach of any settlement or award.
   (c) Disclosing of confidential information.
   (d) Indulgence in any unfair labour practice.
   (e) Changing condition or service in contravention of the Act.
3. Imprisonment up to a period of six months or a fine up to Rs. 500 or both, in event of closure without notice.
4. For violation of any provisions of the act or rules a fine up to Rs. 100.

# The Trade Unions Act, 1926 23

In the year 1926, the Trade Unions Act was passed which happens to be one of the oldest labour legislations in the country. This Act was passed with an objective to provide for the registration of a trade union and to confer upon the registered trade unions certain protection and privileges.

## Trade Union

As per this Act, a trade union is a combination of people formed for the purpose of regulation the relations between:

- employers and the workmen;
- between workmen and workmen; and
- between employers and employers.

## Registration

This legislation provides that seven or more persons in combination can form a trade union. They have to make an application in the prescribed form to the Registrar of Trade Unions. Such application should be accompained with the prescribed registration fees. Along with the application, the applicants are required to submit the name and address of the registered office, a copy of rules of the proposed trade union and particulars of the name and address of its members and officers.

The Registrar of the Trade Union will issue the registration certificate to such a union if he is satisfied that the applicants have complied with all the formalities.

A trade union registered under this Act cannot be registered under the Societies Registration Act, 1860, the Co-operative Societies Act, 1912, or the Companies Act, 1956 and the registration of such trade unions under these Acts is treated as void.

The Registrar of the Trade Union is empowered to withdraw or cancel the registration of a trade union under any of the following circumstances:

(a) If the trade union on its own applies for the cancellation of registration.

(b) If the Registrar is satisfied that the concerned union has obtained the registration by a fraud or mistake.

(c) If due to passage of time the trade union ceases to exist.

(d) If the trade union wilfully contravenes any of the provisions of an Act.

## Rules of a Trade Union

Rules of a trade union are expected to contain at least the following matters:

(1) Name of the trade union.

(2) Objective for which the trade union is established.

(3) Purpose for which the funds of the union will be utilised. These have to be lawful purposes.

(4) Prescribed methods for maintaining the member's list and procedure for inspection by members.

(5) Procedure for admitting the ordinary and Honorary members.

(6) Procedure for payment of subscription by the members. This should not be less than twenty-five paisa per member per month.

(7) Conditions under which the members will receive any benefits under the rules and also under which any fines or penalties that can be imposed on the members.

(8) The method for amendments to the rules.

(9) Methods for appointment of executives and office bearers.

(10) Methods for management of funds, accounts, annual audit and facilities for inspection of the accounts by the members.

(11) Method to dissolve the trade union.

## Legal Position of a Trade Union

In the Act, sections 17 and 19 confer the following legal status to a registered trade union:

1. A trade union registered under the law as a body corporate and therefore has a perpectual succession and common seal.
2. A trade union being a body corporate has powers to acquire and hold both movable and immovable property in its name and also it can enter into contracts with other parties.
3. A trade union can sue other and it can also be sued in its own name.
4. The office bearers and/or memebers of a trade union cannot be prosecuted for a criminal conspiracy for following its legitimate objectives.
5. Against a registered trade union no legal proceedings can be filed in a civil court, in respect of any acts committed in furtherance of a trade dispute even if such as Act:
   (i) induces some other person to break a contract of employment; or
   (ii) is in interference with the trade, business or employment of some other person; or
   (iii) is in interference with the right of some other person to dispose of his capital or his labour at his will. Objects on which the general funds of a Union can be spent:

This Act clearly specifies the list of items on which the trade union funds could be spent. The trade union or its office bearers are not empowered to spend the funds on any other object other than what is prescribed by the law. Purpose for which the funds could be spent for:

(1) Salaries, allowances and expenses of the office bearers.

(2) Expenses for administration of the union.

(3) Legal expenses related to defence or prosecution of the union or its members.

(4) Expenses related to conduct of trade disputes on behalf of the members or that of the union itself.

(5) Compensation to the members for loss arising out of disputes.

(6) Compensation or allowances to the legal heirs of deceased member or to the members on their becoming permanently or partially disabled.

(7) Provision for educational, social or religious benefits for members and their dependents.

(8) Expenses related to periodic publications of the union.

(9) Subject to conditions specified by the Govenment for any other objectives of the trade union.

### Political Fund

A trade union is empowered to constitute a separate fund from separately levied contributions for promoting civil and political interests. This fund is for the following purposes:

(a) Contesting of an election by a candidate for legislative body or civil authority.

(b) Holding of a political meeting in support of a candidate.

(c) Maintenance of a person who is member of legistative body or a local authority.

(d) Registration of electors or selection of candidates.

(e) Holding of political meetings and distribution of political literature and documents.

### General

1. Every member of a trade union and its office bearers have a right to inspect the list of members, books of accounts, etc. at such times as may be provided for this purpose in the rules of trade unions.

2. To be eligible to become an office bearer of a union one must be eighteen years of age and above. He/She must not have been convicted of any offence involving moral turpitude and sentenced to imprisonment unless a period of five years has lapsed since his/her last release from the jail.

3. A person after attaining the age of fifteen years can be admitted as a member of a trade union if the rulers of the concerned trade union permits such admitting of a minor as its member.

4. At least 50% of the office bearers of a trade union must be persons actually engaged or involved in an industry with which the trade union is connected. This means that amongst the office bearers Offences and Penalties:

(1) Punishment by way of a fine up to Rs. 5 can be levied on an office bearer of a union who fails to give any notice or send any statement as required by the Act.

(2) If a person makes a false entry in the union's annual return he can punished with a fine of up to Rs. 500.

(3) With an intention of deceive, if a person gives an incorrect copy of rules of a union to a member or person intending to become a member of the union, he can be punished with a fine of up to Rs. 200.

# The Industrial Employment (Standing Orders) Act, 1946

# 24

The objective of this pre-independence legislation, The Industrial Employment (Standing Orders) Act, 1946 is to ensure that precision the conditions or employment under them and also to make the said conditions known to the workmen employed. It should be noted that the terms and conditions of employment as prescribed under the standing orders would prevail over the corresponding terms in the contract of service/appointment letters.

## Applicability of this Legislation

The Act applies to the whole of India. The law is applicable to every industrial establishment employing hundred or more workmen. However, this Act does not apply to:

(a) Those industries to which the Bombay Industrial Relations Act, 1946, applies, and

(b) To those establishments to which the provisions of the Madhya Pradesh Industrial Employment (Standing Orders) Act, 1961, applies, excepting those which are under the control of the Central Government.

It may be noted that the states of Maharashtra, Gujarat, West Bengal, Karnataka and Tamil Nadu, the Central Government, in respect of union territoris, etc. have extended the provisions of this Act to establishments employing fifty or more workmen.

In case of the state of Tamil Nadu, it is applicable to every factory irrespective of the number of workmen employed if the factory is covered under the Factories Act, 1948. In case of the state of Uttar Pradesh, it can be extended to those establishments employing less that hundred workmen, where the certification of standing orders. It will thus be seen that various states have extended the provisions of this Act in a different manner in respect of their own states.

Definition of "Workmen" in this Act is the same as that of Industrial Disputes Act, 1947.

### Industrial Establishment

In this Act, the definition of the term "Industrial establishment" is very broad. It includes:

(A) Industrial establishment as defined under the Payment of Wages Act, 1936.

(B) A factory, defined under the Factories Act, 1948.

(C) A railway as defined under the Indian Railways Act, 1890.

(D) An establishment of a person, who for the purposes of fulfilling a contract with the owner of any industrial establishment employs workmen.

### Certification of Standing Orders

Every establishment to which this Act applies, the model standing orders, automatically become applicable until such time that the employer does not get his own standing orders certified. The procedure for the certification of standing orders is as under:

(1) Within six months from the date on which this Act becomes applicable to an industrial establishment, the employer is required to submit draft standing orders for his establishment to the certifying officer.

(2) In the draft, the employer is required to make provisions for every matter set out in the schedule of the Act. Wherever the model standing orders are prescribed, the draft should be in conformity with model standing orders as far practicable.

(3) The draft should be accompanied with the particulars of employees engaged in that establishment including the particulars of the trade unions operating therein.

(4) A group of employers is also permitted to submit a common draft for their establishments.

(5) The certifying officer under the Act is authorised to adjudicate upon the fairness or reasonableness of the draft standing orders. If the draft is in conformity with the Act and the rules thereunder and the certifying officer is satisfied with the

reasonableness. He may certify the standing orders in respect of that establishment.

(6) Prior of certification, the certifying officer is expected to forward the draft to the trade unions operating in that establishment and notify the same to all workmen of that establishment in order to hear objections and point of view from 'heir' side, if any. After hearing the parties, i.e., trade unions, workmen and the employer the certifying officer may make changes if necessary and then certify the standing orders.

(7) If the employer is aggrieved by the orders of certifying officer, he has a right to appeal to the prescribed appellate authority for relief. The orders of the appellate authority are final.

(8) Standing orders certified in the above fashion have a binding character on both the workmen and the employer and need to be adopted by the concerned establishment.

It may be noted that there could be deviation in the above procedure from state to state. However, the basic principles are more or less the same. The certified standing orders need to be displayed at a prominent place in the establishment in the English language and also in a language understood by the majority of workmen.

### Payment of subsistence allowance

The Act requires that if an employee is suspended by the employer pending investigation or enquiry into the complaints or charges of misconduct against him, the employer should pay to the workman a subsistence allowance at the following rates:

(a) At the rate of 75% of the wages, as described above for the remaining period of suspension if the delay in the completion of disciplinary proceedings against such a workman is not directly attributable to the conduct of such workman.

However, different State Governments have prescribed various rates of subsistence allowances in respect of this type of suspension in their own model standing orders. An employer can also specify different rates of subsistence allowance in his own certified order, if the rates so prescribed are more beneficial to the workman.

### Matters that need to be provided in the Standing Orders

The schedule of the Act provides a list of matters in respect of which the standing orders can be framed by the employer or the model standing orders by the State Governments. Those standing orders which cover matters other than that are in the schedule are termed as invalid as held in the case of Workman vs. Orissa State Commercial Transport Corporation (1974, 40 C.L.T. 932). The schedule provides for the following matters:

1. Classification of workmen e.g.
   (a) Permanent
   (b) Temporary
   (c) Apprentice
   (d) Probationers
   (e) Badlies, etc.
2. The schedule also provides for the manner in which the employer will communicate to his workmen, matters related to
   (a) Periods and hours of work
   (b) List of holidays
   (c) Pay days
   (d) Wages rates, etc.
3. The schedule also provides that matters related to shift working, attendence, late coming to the work place, etc. can be covered.
4. Conditions of and procedures in applying for the authority which may grant leave and holidays.
5. Requiremnts to enter the premises of the establishment by certain specified gates, liability as regards search of an employee, etc.
6. Closing and reopening of sections of the industrial establishment, and temporary stoppages of work and the rights and liabilities of the employer and workmen arising therefrom.
7. Termination of employment, and the notice thereof to be given by employer and workmen.

8. The schedule provides that provision for suspension or dismissal for misconduct be provided and the acts and ten omissions which constitute the misconduct be also listed.
9. A procedure for the redressal of grievances of the workmen against the unfair treatment or wrongful exactions by the employer or his agents or servants also can be provided in the standing orders.
10. As regards coal mines, additionals matter need to be provided on the following subjects:
    (a) Medical aids in case of an accident.
    (b) Railway travel facilities.
    (c) Methods of filling vacancies.
    (d) Transfer.
    (e) Liability of managers of the establishment of mines.
    (f) Service certificates.
    (g) Exhibition and supply of standing orders.
11. Any other matters that may be prescribed.

(Item listed at point 10 is provided by the Central Government in respect of Union Territories only).

### Offences and Penalties

Various penalties and offences are prescribed by the Act:

1. Failure to submit draft standing orders for certification within the stipulated time on the part of an employer or modification or standing orders without following a prescribed procedure, the recommended punishment is fine up to Rs. 5000 and a further fine of Rs. 200 per day for continuing the offence.
2. For contravention of the certified standing orders by an employer, a fine is prescribed up to Rs. 100 and in case of continuation of the offence a further penalty of Rs. 25 per day.

# Appendices

## APPENDIX-I

## NOTICE UNDER THE INDUSTRIAL DISPUTES ACT, 1947 (ACT XIV OF 1947)

**Synopsis**

1. General
2. Notice of change (section 9-A)
3. Notice to parties (section 10)
4. Notice for terminating award (section 19)
5. Commencement of proceedings by notice (section 20)
6. Notice for strike (section 22)
7. Notice for lock-out (section 22)
8. Notice for retrenchment (section 25-F)
9. Notice for closing (section 25-FFF).
10. Notice for change of hours.
11. Notice to workmen for misconduct, suspension, dismissal and in departmental enquiry.

**1. General.** The Industrial Disputes Act, 1947 (Act XIV of 1947) is an Act to make the provisions for the investigation and settlement of industrial disputes and for certain other purposes.

**2. Notice of change (section 9-A).** Section 9-A of the Industrial Disputes Act, 1947, deals with the provisions relating to notice of change. It makes obligatory on the employer, who proposes to effect any change in the conditions of service applicable to any workmen in respect of any matter specified in the Fourth Schedule, to give notice. The change shall not be effective without giving to the workmen likely to be affected by such change a notice in the prescribed manner of the nature of the change proposed to be effected or, within twenty-one days of giving such notice. The section further provides that no notice shall be required for effecting any such change in the following cases, namely:

(a) where the change is effected in pursuance of any settlement, award or decision of the Appellate Tribunal constituted under the Industrial Disputes (Appellate Tribunal) Act, 1950; or

(b) where the workmen likely to be affected by the change are persons to whom the Fundamental and Supplementary Rules, Civil Services (Classification, Control and Appeal) Rules, Civil Services (Temporary Service) Rules, Revised Leave Rules, Civil Service Regulations, Civilians in Defence Services (Classification, Control and Appeal) Rules, or the Indian Railway Establishment Code or any other rules or regulations that may be notified in this behalf by the appropriate Government in the Official Gazette apply.

**3. Notice to parties (section 10).** Section 10 of the Industrial Disputes Act enacts the provisions relating to reference of disputes to Boards, Courts or Tribunals. It is necessary that in case of reference a notice should be given to all the parties.

**4. Notice for terminating award (section 19).** In River Steam Navigation Company Limited v. Presiding Officer (G. Mehrotra, C.J. and Nayudu and Dutta, JJ), it was held that section 17-A of the Industrial Disputes Act, lays down that an award shall become enforceable on the expiry of thirty days from the date of its publication under section 17 of the said Act. Section 19 (6) of the said Act enacts that notwithstanding the expiry of the period of operation under sub-section (3) of section 19, the award shall continue to be binding on the parties until a period of two months has elapsed from the date on which notice is given by any party bound by the award to the other party or parties intimating its intention to terminate the award. It was further said by their Lordships that apart from the fact that there is no award holding that the workmen were not entitled to claim direct employment, there is nothing in sub-section (6) of section 19, which bars the Government from issuing a fresh notification under section 10 of the said Act. The Legislature under section 19(6) has only made such an award binding on the parties, unless a notice terminating the same is given, but there is nothing in sub-section (6) that it will be binding on the Government and till the award has been terminated by a proper notice, the Government had no power to issue a fresh notification. When the matter comes up before the Tribunal whether the Tribunal will hold that there is no dispute being bound by the earlier award, is a different matter. In cases, it is sufficient to point out, where the agreement itself fixed the period, after expiry of the said period, the settlement becomes inoperative and there is no necessity to give any notice to terminate the settlement. A notice terminating the award need not be in writing.

**5. Commencement of proceedings (section 20).** Section 20 of the Industrial Disputes Act, 1947, deals with the commencement and conclusion of proceedings. It enacts that a conciliation proceeding shall be deemed to have commenced on the date on which a notice of strike or lock-out under section 22 of the said Act is received by the conciliation officer or on the date of the order referring the dispute to a Board, as the case may be.

**6. Notice for strike (section 22).** Section 22 of the Industrial Disputes Act, 1947 deals with the provisions relating to prohibition of strikes and lock-outs. It enacts that the person employed in a public utility service shall not go on strike in breach of contract:

(a) without giving to the employer notice of strike within six weeks before striking; or

(b) within fourteen days of giving such notice; or

(c) before the expiry of the date of strike specified in any such notice as aforesaid; or

(d) during the pendency of any conciliation proceedings before a conciliation officer and seven days after the conclusion of such proceeding.

It is, therefore, extremely essential, that a notice must be given, before the employees or the persons employed in a public utility service go on strike.

**7. Notice for lock-out (section 22).** Regarding lock-out of any public utility service, section 22 of the Industrial Disputes Act, 1947, says that no employer carrying on any public utility service shall lock-out any of his workmen:

(a) without giving them notice of lock-out within six weeks before locking-out; or

(b) within fourteen days of giving such notice; or

(c) before the expiry of the date of lock-out specified in any such notice; or

(d) during the pendency of any conciliation proceedings before a conciliation officer and seven days after the conclusion of such proceedings.

The notice of lock-out or strike shall not be necessary, where there is already in existence a strike or lock-out in the public utility service, but the employer shall send intimation of such lock-out or strike on the day on which it is declared, to such authority as may be specified by the appropriate Government either generally or for a particular area or for a particular class of public utility services.

**8. Notice for retrenchment (section 25-F).** Section 25-F of the Industrial Disputes Act, 1947, deals with the conditions precedent to retrenchment of workman. It enacts that no workman employed in any industry who has been in continuous service for not less than one year under an employer shall be retrenched by that employer until:

(a) the workman has been given one month's notice in writing indicating the reasons for retrenchment and the period of notice has expired, or the workman has been paid in lieu of such notice, wages for the period of the notice, provided that no such notice shall be necessary if the retrenchment is under an agreement which specifies a date for the termination of service;

(b) the workman has been paid, at the time of retrenchment compensation which shall be equivalent to fifteen days' average pay for every completed year of service or any part thereof in excess of six months; and

(c) notice in the prescribed manner is served on the appropriate Government.

In National Iron and Steel Company Limited v. Third Industrial Tribunal (Banerjee, J.), section 25-F provides that no workman shall be retrenched until the condition in question has been satisfied. The conditions of the said section are conditions precedent and are beyond dispute. But still the question remains whether an offer for payment of wages and compensation is equivalent to payment itself and whether by offering such payment in the letter of retrenchment, the conditions precedent should be deemed to have been complied with. Section 25-F of the said Act no doubt says that no workman shall be retrenched "until" he has been given either one month's notice or has been paid, in lieu of such notice, wages for the period of the notice or the workman has been paid compensation calculated under section 25-F (b) of the said Act. But it may be difficult to make a workman accept payment if he will not himself do that. Therefore, an unconditional offer for payment preceding retrenchment, may be equivalent payment.

**9. Notice for closing (section 25-FFF).** Section 25-FFF of the Industrial Disputes Act deals with the provisions relating to compensation to workmen in case of closing down of undertakings. It enacts that where an undertaking is closed down for any reason whatsoever, every workman who has been in continuous service for not less than one year in that undertaking immediately before such closure shall, subject to provisions of sub-section (2) of section 25-FFF of the said Act, be entitled to notice and compensation in accordance with the provisions of section 25-F of the said Act, as if the workman had been retrenched, provided that where the undertaking is closed down on account of unavoidable circumstances beyond the control of the employer, the compensation to be paid to the workman under clause (b) of section 25-F of the said Act shall not exceed his average pay for three months. The explanation attached to sub-section (1) of section 25-FFF of the Industrial Disputes Act enacts that an undertaking which is closed down by reason merely of financial difficulties (including financial losses) or accumulation of undisposed of stock shall not be deemed to have been closed down on account of unavoidable circumstances beyond the control of the employer within the meaning of the proviso to the said sub-section. Sub-section (2) of section 25-FFF of the said section says that where any undertaking set-up for the construction of building, bridges, roads, canals, dams or other construction work is closed down on account of the completion of the work within two years from the date on which the undertaking has been set-up no workman employed therein shall be entitled to any compensation under clause (b) of section 25-F of the said Act, but if the construction work is not so completed within two years, he shall be entitled to notice and compensation under section 25-FFF (1) of the said Act for every completed year of service or any part thereof in excess of six months. A closure in the eye of law cannot be with retrospective effect. But if the closure was due to reasons beyond the control of the businessman, the compensation shall be limited as prescribed by the Proviso, attached to Section 25-FFF(1) of the said Act. Closure of business implies complete stoppage of business. It also discharges the workers thereby.

**10. Notice for change of hours.** In the Associated Cement Staff Union v. The Associated Cement Company Limited Bombay (P.B. Gajendragadkar, K.N. Wanchoo and K.C. Das Gupta, JJ.) it was said by the Supreme Court that it is not the function of industrial adjudication to fix the working hours with an eye to enabling the workmen to earn overtime wages. Hours of work have to be fixed in consideration of many factors including the question of fatigue on the health of the workmen, the effect on their efficiency, the physical discomfort, that may result from long and continuous strain, the need of leisure in the workmen's lives, the hours of work prevailing for similar activities in the same region and also in similar concerns and other relevant factors. But once a conclusion about the normal working hours is reached after considering the optimum working hours on a consideration of all the relevant factors, industrial adjudication cannot hesitate to give effect to its conclusion merely because the workmen would have been entitled to more wages at overtime rates if the hours of work had been fixed at less. While it is true that in fixing the proper wage-scale the question of work-load and so the matter of working hours cannot be left wholly out of consideration many other factors including the need of the workmen, the financial resources of the employer, the rates of wages prevailing in other industries in the region has all to be considered in deciding the wage-scale. It would be against the interests of workmen, the employer and the country as a whole to bring into force wage rates moving on a sliding scale according to the hours of work. The proper solution of the difficulty lies in fixing wage-scales after consideration of all the relevant factors including the working hours and again to fix working hours on a consideration of all relevant factors but without an eye to the effect on the overtime payment of workmen. It is further laid down by the Supreme Court in the said case that it is true that too frequent alterations of conditions of service by industrial adjudication have been generally deprecated for the reasons that it is likely to disturb industrial peace and equilibrium. At the same time, the Supreme Court has more than once pointed out the importance of remembering the dynamic nature of industrial relations. Where conditions of service have been changed only a few years before, industrial adjudication has allowed fresh changes if convinced of the necessity and justification of these by the existing conditions and circumstances.

A notice for change of hours is necessary to be given to the workmen, according to section 9-A of the Industrial Disputes Act. See para No. 2 under the heading "Notice of change (section 9-A)" of this Chapter.

**11. Notice to workmen for misconduct, suspension, dismissal, and the departmental enquiry.** The Supreme Court (P.B. Gajendragadkar, M. Hidayatullah and J.C. Shah, JJ.) said in Meenglas Tea Estate v. The Workmen, that it is an elementary principle that a person who is required to answer a charge must know not only the accusation but also the testimony by which the accusation is supported. He must be given a fair chance to hear the evidence of the witnesses in support of the charge and to put such relevant question by way of cross-examination as he desires. Then he must be given a chance to rebut the evidence led against him. This barest requirement of an enquiry of this character and this requirement must be substantially fulfilled before the result of the enquiry can be accepted. A departure from this requirement in effect throws the burden upon the person charged to repel the charge without first making it out against him.

It was further said by the Supreme Court that in view of the fact that the enquiry was being made into an incident which tock place four-and a-half years ago, in the said case, the Tribunal in assessing the evidence held that it would not accept that any workman was incriminated unless at least two witnesses deposed against him. Some of the workmen got the benefit of this approach and it is now contended that the Tribunal was in error in insisting upon corroboration before accepting the evidence of a single witness. Reference in that connection was made of section 134 of the Indian Evidence Act, 1872 (Act 1 of 1872) which lays down that no particular number of witnesses shall in any case be required for the proof of any fact. It is not a question of error in applying the Evidence Act. It is rather a question of proceeding with caution in a case where admittedly many persons were involved and the incident itself took place, a very long time ago. The Tribunal acted with caution and did not act upon uncorroborated testimony. It is possible, that the evidence against some of the persons to whom the benefit has gone, might be cogent enough for acceptance, but the question is not one of the believing a single witness in respect of any particular workman but of treating all workmen alike and following a method which was likely to eliminate reasonable chances of faulty observation or incorrect recollection. In cases of misconduct, suspension, dismissal or removal, the notices must be drafted in such a manner so that the workmen may grasp the complete things. In departmental enquiries too, the show-cause notice should contain the complete particulars. Rules of natural justice require that a party should have the opportunity of adducing all relevant evidence on which he relies, that the evidence of the opponent should be taken in his presence, and that he should be given the opportunity of cross-examining the witnesses examined by that party, and that no materials should be relied upon against him without his being given an opportunity of explaining them. If these rules are satisfied the enquiry is not open to attack on the ground that the procedure laid down in the Evidence Act was not strictly followed. If after the enquiry the misconduct is proved, the workman is dismissed and is not entitled to any wages for the suspension period, but if the inquiry results in the reinstatement of the workman, he is entitled to full wages for the suspension period also along with reinstatement, unless the employer instead of dismissing the employee can give him a lesser punishment by way of withholding of part of the wages for the suspension period.

When the evidence is oral, normally, the examination of witness will, in its entirety, take place before the party charged, who will have full opportunity of cross-examining him. The position is the same when a witness is called, the statement given previously by him behind the back of the party is put to him, and admitted in evidence, a copy thereof is given to the party, and he is given an opportunity to cross-examine him. To require in that case that the contents of the previous statements should be repeated by the witness word by word and sentence by sentence is to insist on bare technicalities, and rules of natural justice are matters not of form but of substance. It is sufficient compliance when previous statements given by witnesses are read over to them marked on their admission, copies thereof given to the person charged, and he is given an opportunity to cross-examine them. It may be accepted that rules of natural justice do not change from tribunal to tribunal. Even so the purpose of rules of natural justice is to safeguard the position of the person against whom the inquiry is being conducted so that he is able to meet the charge laid against him properly. Therefore, the nature of the inquiry and status of the person against whom the inquiry is being held will have some bearing on what should be the minimum requirements of the rules of natural justice. Where, for example, lawyers are permitted before a tribunal holding an enquiry and the party against whom the inquiry is being held is represented by a lawyer, it may be possible to say that a mere reading of the material to be used in the inquiry may sometimes be sufficient, but where in a domestic inquiry in an industrial matter lawyers are not permitted, something more than a mere reading of statements to be used will have to be required in order to safeguard the interest of the industrial worker. The judicial notice of the fact can be taken that many of the industrial workers are illiterate and sometimes even the representatives of labour union may not be present to defend them. In such a case to read over a prepared statement, in a few minutes and then ask the workmen to cross-examine would make mockery of the opportunity that the rules of natural justice require that the workmen should have to defend themselves. Therefore, when one is taking or dealing with domestic inquiries in industrial matter, the proper course for the management is to examine the witnesses from the begining to the end in the presence of the workman at the inquiry itself. Oral examination always takes such longer time than a mere reading of a prepared statement of the same length and brings home the evidence more clearly to the person against whom the inquiry is being held. Generally, domestic inquiry by the management is to be of this kind. Looking to the illiteracy of the witnesses, and the workmen, it is necessary that the terms of the notice should be simple, and understandable in each and every way.

## APPENDIX-II

## NOTICE UNDER THE TRADE UNIONS ACT, 1926

Form - A

Application for Registration of Trade Union

Form - B

Register of Trade Unions

Form - C

Certificate of Registration of Trade Unions

Form - D

Annual Return prescribed under Section 28 of the Indian Trade Unions Act, 1926, for the year

Ending on 31st March, 19....

Factories Act, 1948 (63 of 1948)

84 [The First Schedule See Section 2 (Cb)]

List for Industries Involving Hazardous

Processes 85 (The Second Schedule)

(See Section 41-F)

Permissible Leaves of Certain Chemical

Substances in Work Environment.

86 (The Third Schedule)

(See Sections 89 and 90)

List for Notifiable Diseases

Notification Issued Under Factories Act

**INDUSTRIAL DISPUTES ACT, 1947**
**70 (FORM - A) (SEE RULE 3)**

Form of Application for the Reference of an Industrial Dispute to a Board of Conciliation.

Form - B

(See Rule - 6)

74 (Form - C)

(See Rule -1)

Form - D

(See Rule-17)

76 a (Form - E)

(See Rule -34)

Form - F

(See Rule - 36)

Form - G

(See rule - 47)

Form of Nomination Paper

77 (Form G-1)

(See Rule 56A)

Form - II

(See Rule - 58)

Form for Memorandum of Settlement

Form - I

(See Rule 59)

Form - J

[See Rule 60(1)]

Form - K

[See Rule 60(2)]

79 (Form K-1)

[See Rule 62(1)]

**APPLICATION UNDER SUB-SECTION (1) OF SECTION 33C OF THE INDUSTRIAL DISPUTES ACT, 1947**

81 (Form K-2)

[See Rule 62(1)]

Application by a person authorised by a workman or by the assignee or heir of a deceased workman under sub-section (1) of Section 33C of the Industrial Disputes Act, 1947,

83 (Form - K 3)

[See Rule 62(2)]

Application by a person who is an assignee or heir of a deceased workman under sub-section (2) of Section 33C of the Industrial Disputes Act, 1947 (14 of 1947)

Form - L

(See Rule 71)

Form of Notices of Strike to be given by 86-87

(Union) in a Public Utility Service

19 (Form - M)

(See Rule 72)

Form of Notice of Lock-out to be given by an Employer Carrying on a public utility service

Form - N

(See rule 73)

Form of Report of Strike or Lock-out in a Public Utility Service

Form - O

(See Rule - 75)

94 (Form - O-1)

(see rule 75A)

96 (Form - O-2)

(See rule 75A)

98 (Form - O-3)

[See rule 75B (1)]

[To be submitted in triplicate 99 (***)]

Form of Application for permission to lay-off to continue the lay-off of workmen in industrial establishments to which provisions of Chapter VB of the Industrial Disputes Act, 1947 (14 of 1947) Apply

Form - P

(See Rule 76)

Form of notice of retrenchment to be given by an employer under clause (C) of Section 25F of the Industrial Disputes Act, 1947

5 (Form PA)

[See Rule 76A (1)]

Form of notice for permission for retrenchment of workmen to be given by an employer under clause (B) of sub-section (1) of section 25N of the Industrial Disputes Act, 1947 (14 of 1947)

[To be made in triplicate 6(***)]

Form PB

9 (Form Q)

(See Rule 76A)

Form of notice of closure to be given by an employer under section 25FFA of the Industrial Disputes Act, 1947

10 (Form QA)

(To be submitted in triplicate)

[See Rule 76C (1)]

Form of notice for permission of closure to be given by an employer under sub-section (1) of Section 25-O of the Industrial Disputes Act, 1947 (14 of 1947)

Form OB

Industrial Tribunal (Central Procedure) Rules, 1954

## APPENDIX-III

## NOTICE UNDER THE INDUSTRIAL EMPLOYMENT (STANDING ORDERS) ACT, 1946

Schedule II

Form I

Industrial Employment (Standing Orders) Act, 1946 - Section 3

Form II

Notice under section 5 of the Industrial Employment (Standing Orders) Act, 1946

Form III

(Industrial Employment (Standing Orders) Act, 1946 - Section 8)

Register - Part I

Industrial Establishment

Part II

(should contain the authenticated copy of the standing orders)

31 (Form IV)

[See rule 74(1)]

To be furnished in respect of each clause appealed against, separately

32 (Form IVA)

(See Standing Order 7A of Schedule 1)

Notice of Discontinuance/Restarting of a shift working to be given by an employer

33 (Form V)

(See Standing Order 1, Schedule IB)

Service Card

## APPENDIX-IV

## NOTICE UNDER THE MINES ACT, 1952

(35 of 1952)

First Schedule Forms

Form - A

[See Rule 48(1)]

Notice of Commencement and of Work

86 (Form B)

[See rules 48(3), 51, 77 and 77A (2)]

Form C

[See rules 48 (3) and 78]

Register of persons employed below ground during the week commencing.........and ending ..........19......

Form D

[See Rules 48 (3) and 78]

Register of persons employed "(above ground) in open cast working during the week commencing.......and ending........19.....

90 (Form E)

[See Rules 48(3) and 78]

Register of persons employed above ground 19 (otherwise than in open cast working) during the week commencing and ending......19............

Form F

[See Rule 49(a)]

Register of Compensatory Days of Rest

Form G

[See Rule 53]

Register of Leave Account during the Calender Year

Form H

(See Rule 53)

Register of Leave Wages Account during the Calender Year

1 (Form-I)

(See Rule 59)

Register of Overtime Wages

1 (Form - J)

2 [See Rule 76(1)]

Return of (Reportable) Accidents

1 (Form - K) [See Rule 76(2)]

Return of Minor Accidents

2 (Form - L) (See rule 54)

Information Regarding Leave with Wages

1 (Form - M)

[See rule 29 D (1)]

Notice of Initial/Periodical Medical Examination under Rule 29B

Form - N

[See rule 29D (3)]

Second and Final Notice of Initial/Periodical Medical Examination under Rule 29B

Form - O

[See rules 29F (1) and 29L]

Medical Standard of Fitness for Persons Employed

Form - P-I

[See rule 29F (1) and 29L]

Medical Standard of Fitness for Persons to be Employed in Mines

Form - Q

[See rule 29J (2) (a)]

Notice of Medical Re-examination by Appellate Medical Board

Form R

[See rule 29J (2) (b)]

Second and Final Notice of Medical Re-examination by Appellate Medical Board

Form S

(See rule 29L)

Report of Medical Re-examination by Appellate Medical Board

Schedule III

[See rule 11(3)]

Minimum Equipment to be kept at the Surface of Mine where no Rescue Room is located close to mine entrance

Schedule IV

[See rule 11(6)]

Adjustments and Test of Breathing Apparatus Flowmeter, Bobin Meter, Oxygen, Etc.

Schedule V

(See Rule 18)

Code of Signs

Schedule VI

(See Rules 20 and 22)

Medical Examination

Schedule VII

(See Rule 21)

Courses of Instructions and Practices

Schedule VIII

[See rule 32(3)]

Code of Signals

## APPENDIX 1

## QUESTIONNAIRE TO EVALUATE A TRAINING PROGRAMME

A. Please circle your most appropriate response in the 5-point scale on the right hand side.

| | | | | | |
|---|---|---|---|---|---|
| 1. The extent to which you were aware of the objectives of the programme at the time of your nomination for this programme. | 1 | 2 | 3 | 4 | 5 |
| 2. The extent to which programme objectives were explained at the commencement of the programme. | | | | | |
| 3. The extent to which the programme objectives were fulfilled | | | | | |

| | 1 | 2 | 3 | 4 | 5 |
|---|---|---|---|---|---|
| 4. The extent to which the objective of the programme was in line with your need. | | | | | |
| 5. The extent to which your need was satisfied. | | | | | |
| 6. The participant mix for the programme was | 1<br>very bad | 2<br>bad | 3<br>good | 4<br>V.Good | 5<br>Ideal |
| 7. The duration of the programme was | 1<br>too less | 2<br>less | 3<br>just right | 4<br>much | 5<br>too much |
| 8. Do you agree that the programme would have been more beneficial if some more background material would have been sent in advance? | 1<br>Strongly agree | 2<br>Agree | 3<br>Difficult to say | 4<br>Little | 5<br>Not at all |
| 9. The relative coverage of various topics was | 1<br>highly inadequate | 2<br>inade-quate | 3<br>average | 4<br>sufficient | 5<br>ideal |
| 10. How well was the programme organised? | 1<br>Very badly | 2<br>Badly | 3<br>Well | 4<br>Very well | 5<br>Excep-tionally well |
| 11. Usefulness of the programme in direct work situation. | 1 | 2 | 3 | 4 | 5 |
| 12. Usefulness of the programme in indirect work situation. | 1 | 2 | 3 | 4 | 5 |
| 13. Usefulness of the programme in off-the-highly inadequate | 1 | 2 | 3 | 4 | 5 |
| 14. Usefulness of the programme in developing others. | 1 | 2 | 3 | 4 | 5 |
| 15. Usefulness of the programme in long-term. | 1 | 2 | 3 | 4 | 5 |
| 16. Usefulness of the programme in personnel growth and development. | 1 | 2 | 3 | 4 | 5 |

B. Kindly respond to the following questions in the space provided against them. You may use separate sheets, if required:

(i) How was your nomination made for this programme?

(ii) How much in advance you were informed of your nomination?

(iii) What was your expectation from this programme?

(iv) What should be the objective of these programmes?

(v) What are the reasons for the non-fulfilment of the programme objectives?

(vi) Kindly enumerate three important gains to you from this programme.

(vii) Kindly enumerate the topics/session needing more coverage and specify the duration wanted.

(viii) Kindly enumerate the topics/sessions which have been given coverage/time more than desired (please indicate the appropriate durations).

(ix) Kindly enumerate the topics/sessions you would like to be omitted.

(x) Any other suggestions for improving the programme.

## APPENDIX 2

## HRD CLIMATE QUESTIONNAIRE

This questionnaire developed by Centre for HRD at the Xavier Labour Relations Institute, Jamshedpur, has 38 statements.

The employees/officers have to give their assessment of the HRD climate in their organisation by rating their organisation on each statement using 5-point scale in the following manner:

'5' - 'A' rating of 5 indicates that the statement is 'almost always true';

'4' - 'A' rating of 4 indicates that the statement is 'mostly true';

'3' - 'A' rating of 3 indicates that the statement is 'sometimes true';

'2' - 'A' rating of 2 indicates that the statement is 'rarely true';

and

'1' - 'A' rating of 1 indicates that the statement is 'not at all true'.

### Questionnaire on HRD Climate Developed by the Centre for HRD at the XLRI

| | 5 | 4 | 3 | 2 | 1 |
|---|---|---|---|---|---|
| 1. The top management of this organisation goes out of its way to make sure that employees enjoy their work. | | | | | |
| 2. The top management believes that human resources are extremely important resources and that they have to be treated more humanely. | | | | | |

| | 5 | 4 | 3 | 2 | 1 |
|---|---|---|---|---|---|
| 3. Development of the subordinates is seen as an important part of their job by the managers/officers here. | | | | | |
| 4. The personnel policies in this organisation facilitate employee development. | | | | | |
| 5. The top management is willing to invest a considerable part of its time and other resources to ensure the development of employees. | | | | | |
| 6. Senior officers/executives in this organisation take active interest in their juniors and help them learn their job. | | | | | |
| 7. People lacking competence in doing their jobs are helped to acquire competence rather than being left unattended. | | | | | |
| 8. Managers in this organisation believe that employee's behaviour can be changed and people can be developed at any stage of their life. | | | | | |
| 9. People in this organisation are helpful to each other. | | | | | |
| 10. Employees in this organisation are very informal and do not hesitate to discuss their personal problems with their supervisors. | | | | | |
| 11. The psychological climate in this organisation is very conducive for any employee interested in developing himself by acquiring new knowledge and skills. | | | | | |
| 12. Seniors guide their juniors and prepare them for future responsibilities/roles they are likely to take up. | | | | | |
| 13. The top management of this organisation makes efforts to identify and utilise the potential of the employees. | | | | | |
| 14. Promotion decisions are based on the suitability of the promotee rather than on favouritism. | | | | | |
| 15. There are mechanisms in this organisation to reward any good work done or any contribution made by employees. | | | | | |
| 16. Performance appraisal reports in this organisation are based on objective assessment and adequate information and not on favouritism. | | | | | |
| 17. When an employee does good work his supervising officers take special care to appreciate it. | | | | | |

18. People in this organisation do not have any fixed mental impressions about each other. 5 4 3 2 1
19. Employees are encouraged to experiment with new methods and try out creative ideas.
20. When any employee makes a mistake his super-visors treat it with understanding and help him to learn from such mistakes rather than punish him or discourage him.
21. Weaknesses of employees are communicated to them in a non-threatening way.
22. When behaviour feedback is given to employees they take seriously and use it for development.
23. Employees in this organisation take pains to find out their strengths and weakness from their supervising officers or colleagues.
24. When employees are sponsored for training, they take it seriously and try to learn from the programmes they attend.
25. Employees returning from training programmes are given opportunities to try out what they have learnt.
26. Employees are sponsored for training programmes on the basis of genuine training needs.
27. People trust each other in this organisation.
28. Employees are not afraid to express or discuss their feelings with their supervisors.
29. Employees are not afraid to express or discuss their feelings with their subordinates.
30. Employees are encouraged to take initiative and do things on their own without having to wait for instructions from supervisors.
31. Delegation of authority to encourage juniors to develop handling higher responsibilities is quite common in this organisation.
32. When seniors delegate authority to juniors the juniors use it as an opportunity for development.
33. Team spirit is of high order in this organisation.
34. When problems arise people discuss them openly and try to solve thorn rather than keep accusing each other behind their backs.
35. Career opportunities are pointed out to juniors by senior officers in the organisation.

| | | | | | | |
|---|---|---|---|---|---|---|
| 36. | The orgnisation's future plans are made known to the managerial staff to help them develop their juniors and prepare them for the future. | 5 | 4 | 3 | 2 | 1 |
| 37. | This organisation ensures employee welfare to such an extent that the employees can save a lot of their mental energy for work purposes. | | | | | |
| 38. | Job rotation in this organisation facilitates employee development. | | | | | |

## APPENDIX 3

## SIMPLIFIED QUESTIONNAIRE — MORALE OF EXECUTIVES

| Sl. No. | Questions | Response: Yes | Sometimes | No |
|---|---|---|---|---|
| 1. | Do you think that the management is fair in its dealings with the executives? | | | |
| 2. | Do you feel that the executives have a pride of place in the organisation? | | | |
| 3. | Do you feel that the management is fair with the executives in matters of pay scales and perks? | | | |
| 4. | Do you feel that deputation for training is generally done impartially in your organisation? | | | |
| 5. | Do you feel that you have the management support when you take some emergency decisions depending on the exigency of a situation? | | | |
| 6. | Do you feel that your present reporting and status are justified in keeping with your attainments? | | | |
| 7. | Do you have access to your works manager and chief executive for your personal matters of importance? | | | |
| 8. | Do you feel that the management is giving you sufficient opportunity for career growth? | | | |
| 9. | Do the promotions go to the deserving people in all fairness and giving due weightage to qualifications, experience and competence? | | | |
| 10. | Do you feel that good work is recognised by the management and is duly rewarded? | | | |
| 11. | Do you feel that the management is following a rational promotion policy? | | | |

| Sl. No. | Questions | Response | | |
|---|---|---|---|---|
| | | Yes | Sometimes | No |
| 12. | Do you feel satisfied with your reportability and responsibility? | | | |
| 13. | Do you feel that you are utilising your knowledge and ability in your job? | | | |
| 14. | Do you feel that you have been given adequate authority/power to handle your workers? | | | |
| 15. | Do you feel that there is proper motivation for putting your best efforts in your assignment? | | | |
| 16. | Do the management feel that the executives should be successful leaders of their subordinates? | | | |
| 17. | Do you find that your boss is competent to guide your activities? | | | |
| 18. | Is intentional by-passing of the immediate officers discouraged by your superiors? | | | |
| 19. | Do you feel that the executives in middle management are given a chance to participate in vital decision-making? | | | |
| 20. | Do you feel that there is no communication gap in your organisation? | | | |
| 21. | Do you feel that the management considers your grievances and suggestions seriously? | | | |
| 22. | Do you feel that your boss is encouraging you for better work and is not in the habit of finding faults in your work? | | | |
| 23. | Do you feel that you should stick to your present organisation and should not join elsewhere to better your prospects? | | | |
| 24. | Do you feel a sense of belonging for the company? | | | |
| 25. | Do you feel that your family will be well protected by the company and given all help in rehabilitating themselves in case of your permanent disablement or death while on duty? | | | |

*Note*: Here the questionnaire (which is meant to be indicative only) has been worded in a manner to facilitate analysis and direct measurement. The rating could be done as under:

| *Average number of affirmatives* | *Rating* |
|---|---|
| 20 and above | Very High Morale |
| 16 to 20 | Good Morale |
| 11 to 15 | Average Morale |
| 10 and below | Low Morale |

It is important that sample size and random distribution of questionnaires should be ensured. A fair cross-section should be covered without any bias.

For purposes of score 'sometimes' can be considered as 50% 'Yes' and 50% No.

## APPENDIX 4

## QUESTIONNAIRE FOR STAFF SUPERVISORY TRAINING NEEDS SURVEY

### Part I

Consider each of the following topics and indicate whether or not additional training is needed. Check one response for each topic. (Supervisors should answer in terms of their own needs and those of other supervisors they know well. Managers should answer in terms of their own needs and those of supervisors reporting to them.)

Space is also provided for specific comments regarding the nature of the problem involved and/or the type of training that would be most appropriate. Such comments are particularly encouraged wherever the 'Yes' column is checked. Indicate the number of the topics referred to.

| Topic | Training Recommended | | Comments |
|---|---|---|---|
| | Yes | No | |
| 1. Organisation and function of major company components | | | |
| 2. Functions of plant and division staff activities (Labour Relations, Controller, Plant Engineering, etc.) | | | |
| 3. Line-staff relationships | | | |
| 4. Interviewing job applicants | | | |
| 5. Making the selection decision | | | |
| 6. Position classification system | | | |
| 7. Salary administration | | | |

## Part II

Many specialised short courses and seminars of interest to management personnel are offered by various management and professional associations as well as colleges and universities. These courses are intensive and comprehensive programmes of study and of application in specific subject areas and generally involve eight to forty clock hours per topic.

A. The following list is a representative sample of possible topics for such specialised short courses. Review this list and check any you would be interested in attending, if offered by the company (space is provided for suggesting additional topics):

1. The functions and Goals of Management: Trends and Problems
2. Data and Decision: The use of Electronic Computers in Industry
3. Principles and Techniques of Interviewing
4. Understanding the Problems of Production Supervision
5. Application of Scientific Method in Solving Business Problems
6. Stimulating Employee Creativity
7. Market Research Activities
8. Effective Public Speaking
9. Supervising the Professional Employee
10. Operations Research Methods
11. Work Standards
12. Time Management
13. Labour-Management Relationship
14. The Decision-making Process
15. Recent Research Findings in Industrial Relations
16. Effective Report Writing
17. Manufacturing Automation
18. Human Relations in Industry
19. Company Research and Development Activities
20. Selection of Supervisory Personnel
21. Performance Appraisal

22. Information Theory Applied to Modern Physics and Engineering
23. Quality Control
24. Statistical Methods in Industry
25. The Design and Analysis of Industrial Experiments
26. Managing Product Engineering
27. The Future Growth of the National Economy
28. Quality of Work Life
29. Business Gaming: Simulating Managerial Decisions
30. Interpersonal Communications
31. Speed Reading

B. Review the topics you checked in question 1 above. Rank them in order of importance:

(a) First choice

(b) Second choice

(c) Third choice

C. Consider the topic you ranked as your first choice. Would you regard it to be of sufficient importance and value to justify attending it during normal working hours? Yes/No.

D. Check your present classification:

(1) Manager (2) Supervisor (3) Other (specify)

*Note*: This questionnaire should not be answered by supervisors of production. A separate form is available for them.

## FORM-B QUESTIONNAIRE

Write the answer that best applies to you at the left of the statement.

A. Each of the following statements can be answered in any one of these alternatives:

| | | |
|---|---|---|
| Never | = | 0 |
| Rarely | = | 1 |
| Occasionally | = | 2 |
| Sometimes | = | 3 |
| Often | = | 4 |
| Usually | = | 5 |

1. I try to be with people.
2. I let other people decide what to do.
3. I join social groups.
4. I try to have close relationship with people.
5. I tend to join social organisations when I have an opportunity.
6. I let other people strongly influence my actions.
7. I try to be included in informal social activities.
8. I try to have close, personal relationships with people.
9. I try to include other people in my actions.
10. I let other people control my actions.
11. I try to have people around me.
12. I try to get close and personal with people.
13. When people are doing things together I tend to join them.
14. I am easily led by people.
15. I try to avoid being alone.
16. I try to participate in group activities.

B. Each of the following statements can be answered in any one of these alternatives:

| | | |
|---|---|---|
| No body | = | 0 |
| One or two people | = | 1 |
| A few people | = | 2 |
| Some people | = | 3 |
| Many people | = | 4 |
| Most people | = | 5 |

17. I try to be friendly with people.
18. I let other people decide what to do.
19. My personal relations with people are cool and distant.
20. I let other people take charge of things.
21. I try to have close relationships with people.
22. I let people strongly influence my actions.
23. I try to get close and personal with people.
24. I let other people control my actions.
25. I act cool and distant with people.

26. I am easily led by people.
27. I try to have close, personal relationships with people.
28. I like people to invite me to things.
29. I like people to act close and personal with me.
30. I try to influence strongly other people's actions.
31. I like people to invite me to join in their activities.
32. I like people to act close towards me.
33. I try to take charge of things when I am with people.
34. I like people to include me in their activities.
35. I like people to act cool and distant toward me.
36. I try to have others do things the way I want them done.
37. I like people to ask me to participate in their discussions.
38. I like people to act friendly toward me.
39. I like people to invite me to participate in their activities.
40. I like people to act distant toward me.

C. Each of the following statements can be answered in any one of these alternatives:

| | | |
|---|---|---|
| Never | = | 0 |
| Rarely | = | 1 |
| Occasionally | = | 2 |
| Sometimes | = | 3 |
| Often | = | 4 |
| Usually | = | 5 |

41. I try to dominate people when I am with people.
42. I like people to invite me to things.
43. I like people to act close toward me.
44. I try to have other people do things the way I want them done.
45. I like people to invite me to join in their activities.
46. I like people to act cool and distant toward me.
47. I try to influence strongly other people's actions.
48. I like people to include me in their activities.
49. I like people to act close and personal with me.

50. I try to take charge of things when I'm with people.
51. I like people to invite me to participate in their activities.
52. I like people to act distant toward me.
53. I try to have other people do things the way I want them done.
54. I take charge of things when I am with people.

A respondent's scores for different kinds of needs can be calculated with the help of the following key:

| | |
|---|---|
| Need for inclusion | Expressed (see answers to statements 1, 3, 5, 7, 9, 11, 13, 15 and 16) Wanted (see answers to statements 28, 31, 34, 37, 39, 42, 45, 48 and 51) |
| Need for control | Expressed (see answers to statements 30, 33, 36, 41, 44, 47, 50, 53 and 54) Wanted (see answers to statements 2, 6, 10, 14, 18, 20, 22, 24 and 26) |
| Need for affection | Expressed (see answers to statements 4, 8, 12, 17, 19, 21, 23, 25 and 27) Wanted (see answers to statements 29, 32, 35, 38, 40, 43, 46, 49 and 52) |

## APPENDIX 5

## PERFORMANCE APPRAISAL

*Note*: Please place a tick (✓) under any one of the six degrees which correctly represents your view about each statement:

| | Very High | Quite High | Rather High | Rather Low | Quite Low | Very Low |
|---|---|---|---|---|---|---|
| 1. My satisfaction with the appraisal system is: | | | | | | |
| 2. My Knowledge about the exact appraisal rating for me is: | | | | | | |
| 3. The probability of my appraisal being done exclusively by my immediate superior is: | | | | | | |
| 4. The extent of closeness between my formal appraisal rating done by the organisation and my self-assessment usually is: | | | | | | |
| 5. My knowledge of criteria used in my performance appraisal is: | | | | | | |

| | Very High | Quite High | Rather High | Rather Low | Quite Low | Very Low |
|---|---|---|---|---|---|---|
| 6. The extent of closeness between my formal appraisal rating and the corresponding monetary rewards is: | | | | | | |
| 7. The link between annual appraisals and the development of new or better job-related qualities and skills for me is: | | | | | | |
| 8. Frequency of formal feedback and guidance to me before the annual appraisal, about my performance is: | | | | | | |
| 9. The ability of the current formal appraisal system to reflect my superior's real assessment of me is: | | | | | | |
| 10. The possibility of unbiased assessment of my performance relative to that of my colleagues under the present system is: | | | | | | |
| 11. Help rendered by annual appraisal getting more appropriate jobs, placements, etc., for me is: | | | | | | |
| 12. My feeling of being placed under the right boss is: | | | | | | |
| 13. In my view the extent of parity between relative levels of performance standards among various deptts./regions/functions is: | | | | | | |
| 14. The degree of mutual understanding in my work relationships with my superior is: | | | | | | |
| 15. The need for formal appraisals for employees like me is: | | | | | | |
| 16. The extent of fairness of the review of the appraisals done by my superior's superior is: | | | | | | |
| 17. The extent of effort in discovering my potential for higher responsibility through my appraisals is: | | | | | | |
| 18. The extent of action taken by the organisation to assist me in fulfilling the potentials discovered is: | | | | | | |

| | Very High | Quite High | Rather High | Rather Low | Quite Low | Very Low |
|---|---|---|---|---|---|---|
| 19. The extent of detailed discussion and guidance for future performance on the basis of past year's performance appraisal is: | | | | | | |
| 20. The extent of opportunity provided to air my frank opinions, views and problems during discussion of my appraisal is: | | | | | | |
| 21. The appropriateness of the procedure whereby the superior's superior reviews my appraisal is: | | | | | | |
| 22. The time spent on such discussion usually is: | | | | | | |
| 23. The extent of satisfaction derived by me through participating in the appraisal discussion with my superiors is: | | | | | | |

24. (a) In my experience at present the discussion on my appraisal centres around: (please rank the following with 1 for the most significant item, 2 for the next most important and so on, until 7 for the least. Put the number in the box provided on the right)

(i) My past period's job performance levels ☐
(ii) My personal strengths ☐
(iii) My future performance levels ☐
(iv) My salary/promotion ☐
(v) My training or learning needs ☐
(vi) My personal weaknesses ☐
(vii) My problems and difficulties ☐

(b) In my opinion the ideal ranking in order of importance of the factors in 24(a) should be:

(i)
(ii)
(iii)
(iv)
(v)
(vi)
(vii)

# APPENDIX 6

## SAMPLE OF AN EMPLOYEE SUGGESTION SCHEME

### Suggestion Scheme

Suggester's name Personal No.

Father's name Designation

Department Section

Main features of the scheme:
(Give details of suggestion)
sketch/drawing etc.

How do you assess that it will contribute to the efficiency/cost saving/or any other improvement? If economic results are anticipated, please give calculations.

Date Full signature of suggestor

To be filled in triplicate. First copy to the Head of the Department. Second copy to be given to the Secretary Suggestion Scheme and the third copy to be retained as office copy by the suggestor.

(*Please use a separate sheet if space is insufficient*)

**NOT TO BE FILLED BY THE SUGGESTOR**

Date of receipt: Put up for examination on:

Decision of the committee:

Remarks/approval of Secretary/
Chairman, Suggestion Committee
Results communicated to the Suggestor on:

Secretary
Suggestion Scheme

# Bibliography


Balu, V. Human Resource Development, Sri Venkateswara Publications, Madras, 1934.

Banerjee, A.M. & Prasad, Lallan. Management of Human Resources, Sterling Publishers Pvt. Ltd., New Delhi, 1955.

C.B. Mamoria & S. Mamoria. 'Dynamics of Industrial Relations in India, Himalaya Publishing House, Mumbai, 1995.

Craig, R.L. A Handbook of Training and Development, McGraw-Hill, New York, 1976.

D. Yoder. Personnel Management and Industrial Relations, Prentice Hall India Ltd., New Delhi, 1972.

Dayal, Ishwar. Management Training in Organisation, Prentice-Hall of India Pvt. Ltd., New Delhi, 1970.

Ghosh, Subratesh. Personnel Management; Oxford & IBH Publishing Company, New Delhi, 1985.

Houstan, G.D. Manager Development: Principles and Perspectives Homewood, Illinosis, R.D. Irwin In., 1961.

J.T. Dunlop. Industrial Relations Systems, New York, H. Holt and Co. 1958.

Johnson, S.R. TQM: Leadership for the Quality Transformation (Jan. 1993); Book Abstracts in Quality Progress.

M.L. Chandak. 'Law of Notices', Law Book Company, Allahabad, 1969.

M.W. Reder. Labour in a Growing Economy, New York, John Wiley and Sons, Inc. 1957.

McGehee, W. and Thayer, P.W. Training in Business and Industry John Wiley & Sons, New York, 1961.

National Commission on Labour Report, New Delhi, Manager of Publications, Government of India, 1969.

P. Suffa Rao & N. Narayana. "Quality of Worklife" cited in 'The Indian Journal of Labour Economics' Vol. XXXII, No. 1, April, 1989. CII: "Training Manual on ISO 9000".

Papers presented at the National HRD Network Conference on the 'Changing Role of Human Resource Development in the New Economic Environment': January 20-22, 1994, Bombay.

Patten, T.H. Development of Human Resources and Manpower Planning; Wiley, New York, 1971.

Rao, P.K. A Guide to ISO 9000 Registration (1993).

Rao, T.V., Silveiram D.M., Srivastava, C.M., Vidyasagar Rajesh (Editors). HRD in the New Economic Environment; Tata McGraw-Hill, New Delhi, 1995.

Richard E. Walton. Quality of Working Life: What is it? Sloan Management Review, Fall 1973.

S.L. Agarwal. Labour Relations Law in India, New Delhi, MacMillan Co. of India Ltd. 1978.

Safety Study Manual, Vol. IV. Institute of Miner's and Metal Worker's Education, Dhanbad, 1997.

Subratesh Ghosh. 'Personnel Management', Oxford & IBH Publishing Company, New Delhi, 1985.

Subratesh Ghosh. Trade Unionism in Underdeveloped Countries, Calcutta, Book Land Pvt. Ltd. 1960.

Tripathi, P.C. Human Resource Development; S. Chand & Sons, New Delhi, 1997.

Vivek Paranjpe. 'Human Resource Management in India - Legal Perspective; Capital Books International, New Delhi, 1991.

### Journals Referred

Harvard Business Review, Harvard University.

Human Resources Management, Michigan University.

Indian Journal of Industrial Relations, Shri Ram Centre for Industrial Relations, New Delhi.

Indian Journal of Labour Economics, Indian Society of Labour, Lucknow.

Indian Journal of Training and Development, Indian Society for Training and Development, New Delhi.

Indian Labour Journal, Indian Labour Bureau, Simla.

Indian Management, All India Management Association, New Delhi.

International Labour Review, Geneva.

Management and Labour Studies - XLRI, Jamshedpur.

### Bare Acts

Industrial Disputes Act, 1947.

Industrial Employment (Standing Order) Act, 1946.

Trade Union Act, 1926.

# Index